Nobody's Baby

Teresa J. Carson

Sugarbaby Books
USA

This book is a work of fiction. All names, characters, locations, events, and situations come from the author's imagination. Any resemblance to real people is coincidental.

Copyright © 2019 Teresa J. Carson

Cover art by Mary Bruno, PhD

Library of Congress certificate of registration

Summary: In the Great Smoky Mountains near Cherokee land, Nikki's junior year of high school ends with an unchaperoned pool party that also ends her innocence.

ISBN–13: 978-0-9858264-5-1

1st book edition, July, 2019

www.sugarbabybooks.com

Published in the USA by Sugarbaby Books

In memory of my precious son, Chip Verling,
and the precious children at
St. Jude Children's Research Hospital
in Memphis, Tennessee

My Garden of Prayer

My garden beautifies my yard

    and adds fragrance to the air…

But it is also my cathedral

    and my quiet place of prayer…

So little do we realize that

    the glory and the power

Of He who made the universe

    lies hidden in a flower.

—Helen Steiner Rice

Contents

Prologue

My dream

A faceless mob surrounded me in a dark, dense forest. They pointed, yelled, and shook their fists. Two of them grabbed my arms and dug their grubby fingernails into my skin. The maddened crowd huffed and puffed sour breath into my face as they shoved me into a small wooden shack.

Layers of latent dust rose into the air and choked me. I gasped for breath, but the mob showed no mercy. They pushed and pulled me as if I were a rag doll.

In my mind, I struggled and tried to wriggle free, but my arms and legs wouldn't obey. Some disconnect prevented my body from defending itself; I was lost to the resolve of this angry horde.

At first, I couldn't understand their anger, then someone shouted, "Lock her up! She was bitten! Nikki has rabies!"

I don't remember a bite.

Rough men pinned my shoulders to the timber-slatted wall, and one wrapped a rope around my throat. I told my feet to kick, but they wouldn't move. I told my fingers to scratch, but they fell limp and dangled from sweaty palms.

Involuntarily, I coughed, gagged, and threw up.

"Dammit!" yelled a man, wiping vomit from his cheek.

Backing away, the crowd retreated in fear of catching the

rabies virus. They barred the rustic door and sealed me inside the dusty, run-down shed. Shouting obscenities as they ran, the enraged pack scattered through the shadowy forest like a colony of insects escaping from a trampled ant hill.

Just as the loose line dropped from my neck, I shuddered and started to tremble with agonizing pain. Was it true? Was I bitten by a rabid animal?

Is this what rabies feels like… like a writhing, wild animal twisting inside?

The virus or whatever was taking over smacked me against the rough-hewn boards then slammed me to the grimy floor. A thousand splinters zoomed into the air and fused into larger wooden shards. The fragments swooped down and penetrated my body with determined force.

I protested the assault with uncontrollable convulsions. Still, my mind and body did not communicate or work together. I was unable to fight back at will.

Think, Nikki, think! I must detach from this brutal assault. I must concentrate on calm images.

While pretending to glide in pleasant blue skies and to float on frothy white clouds, I imagined a misty haze showering my body with gentle rain. Within the warm spray, a gusty breeze emerged and lifted me into a brimming butterfly bush. In my vision, I saw hundreds of soft, yellow butterflies taking flight.

Then, drifting back down, one by one, the tiny creatures tickled my skin as they landed, and I smiled until…

Peace. Joyful tranquility. The attack on my body had ended abruptly. I expelled a sigh of relief and hoped the rabid disease had vacated these innocent woodlands.

Lying still on the cold, hard floor, I peered through the

cracks of the wide-planked walls and studied the silent fog that meandered along the forest floor.

Morning sunbeams sliced into the shack and warmed my battered body. Brown bunnies hopped from plant to plant, honey bees siphoned nectar from rising yellow crocus, and magically, the ramparts of my stockade fell away.

Chapter One – Chaos

Looking back on May 29th

I awoke and bolted into a sitting position. Arrows of hot sun struck my face. Sticky leaves clung to my exposed body, scrapes and bruises wallpapered my arms and legs, and my bikini top and bottom were hanging by a thread. How long had I been lying in the forest?

Gradually, the earthy scents of tree bark and pine needles cleared my head, and in a flash, I remembered a disturbing dream. Dismissing the nightmare, I shook my head, took a deep breath, and pieced together the events that put me here.

On Friday night, Charlie Quinn's wild, last-day-of-school pool party had ended as soon as his parents arrived unexpectedly. My friends and I and the others dashed into the dark woods of the Great Smoky Mountains behind his house. The forecasted full moon hid behind storm clouds and failed to light a path for us.

Running blind, through the tall white pines that grow on the east side of the foothills, we laughed at first. However, the minute people started tripping over fallen limbs, stumps, and large rocks, chaotic screams echoed through the forest. The escaping teens elbowed each other like people running with the bulls in Spain.

As I ran deeper into the woods, branches of maple and sweet gum trees smacked my face with new spring leaves, and my eyes stung from sweat mixed with the dust of freshly trampled dirt.

Then, I recalled falling.

While scrambling up and down the hilly terrain, I had plummeted into a deep ravine... rolling, rolling... until everything went black.

As I tried to remember more, I wiped the matted hair from my cheeks, rubbed my eyes, and crawled to my knees to test my balance. Judging by the puddled water and freshly snapped tree limbs, rain had poured during the night.

With gritty eyes, I squinted at the mocking sun. It was one of those warm mornings that should make a person glad to be alive... yet, here I was, wobbling to my feet, alone, wet, and dirty in these eerily silent woods.

No birds sang; no squirrels skittered up and down trees; no rabbits foraged for tender shoots.

Feeling a tickle above my eye, I touched my aching head, drew back a red-stained finger, and shrieked at the congealed blood. Did I hit a boulder or a tree when I fell?

Hoping to get home before my parents missed me, I put one foot in front of the other and regained my stability.

Dad and Bogey, my little brother, had taken their horses on an overnight trail ride, and my mom was visiting her sister in Asheville. They would be getting back late.

Combing through the undergrowth, I hunted for the clothes I had grabbed from the pool deck. Plastered on a blackberry bush that clung to the side of the gorge, my jeans and shirt had shape-shifted into the likeness of a stuffed scarecrow. I grinned at the cornfield figure, even though my back tweaked from lying on the ground all night, and my shoulders sagged like great grandmother's.

The cell phone still neatly stashed in my pants pocket showed no calls or texts. My friends probably thought I made it home okay… unless… they had fallen, too.

"Carly? Gary? Anyone?" I yelled, but no one answered.

Carly, my best friend and confidante stirred up trouble sometimes, which was exciting to me since I'm basically shy… over protected, she would say.

I could just hear Carly challenging me or urging me out of my comfort zone. "Come on, Nikki!"

Once, she got us into a girl fight with older, out-of-town bullies. Luckily, some guys that Carly knew from another county showed up and pulled the girls off. Carly had a knack for meeting people.

Chuckling softly, I pictured the petite sixteen-year-old swinging her dark-brown ponytail. Carly's tiger eyes had danced with delight when she blurted Charlie Quinn's secret. "He's having a pool party while his parents are away for their older son's graduation."

A sudden, chilly gust of wind brought my thoughts back to the forest and a gnawing realization: I didn't know exactly where I was.

My eyelids quivered, leaves fluttered, and I shuddered.

With the breeze, woodsy aromas of new green moss, tree sap, and rain-soaked earth wafted through the air. *But now, those same smells that I loved as a child would remind me of this day. Which way is my house?*

Confused, I imagined being lost, and nightmarish predators creeped into my mind.

I pulled on my jeans, tucked in my shirt, and searched for

my sneakers. Oddly, six feet away and turned upside down in a narrow stream, one shoe was surrounded by footprints.

Puzzled, I stretched the wet shoe onto my bruised foot and shuffled through a blanket of fallen leaves to look for the other one. In a thicket of chokeberry bushes, something unsettling caught my eye.

The toe of a boy's high-top tennis shoe jutted from behind an old log. I lifted the large, black shoe and was shocked to see my grey sneaker almost buried in soft red mud.

After looking in every direction for any other signs of people, I felt that something was out of sync. So, I left the boy's shoe where I found it.

Nothing made sense. If someone fell into the ravine with me, why didn't he help me?

Still lightheaded and groggy, I scrambled out of the gulch and tried to get my bearings. On this mountainous terrain, homes were usually nestled on five-acre wooded lots, but I didn't see any structures at all. I listened for sounds of cars, horses, or children, but the twitter of birds was all I heard.

Thinking my house couldn't be that far, I walked east, toward the sun, and remembered what had happened the night before.

The pool party had rocked strong for an hour or two. My friends and I danced and swam while loud music blasted. In addition to his friends at school, Charlie had invited his older cousins from Ashville and a few kids from Qualla Boundary, the land of the Eastern Band of Cherokee Indians, which bordered our town.

Most of the guys I had never met, and some stared rudely at Carly and me. One boy with slick, dark hair, a smooth olive complexion, and piercing brown eyes, captured my attention. His striking face had high cheek bones and a serious expression. I heard the others call him Wolfie the dreamer, because he was quiet. I smiled shyly at him.

Wolfie played quarterback at Cherokee High School and dated an older girl who was away at college. Why was I drawn to Wolfie when I thought I was in love with Joey Paul Haute?

Joey Paul was captain of the JFK High School football team and had been accepted to Duke University next year. I had chased him for two years and purposely put myself in his path every chance I got. Learning his schedule, I would stroll past his classes when the bell rang and hoped he would notice me. After lunch, I walked down the stairs that he came up.

Joey Paul knew I was alive alright. He had asked me to dance a couple of times at after-game mixers, but recently, he seemed to avoid me.

At the party, Joey Paul stood aloof with his friends while I stole glances at his muscular, six-foot body. The sandy-brown hair on his Greco-Roman head looped into soft curls, daring me to run my fingers through it. I fantasized that his bright blue eyes would soon meet my blue-green ones until…

"Nikki Loveleigh, wanna dance?" Gary, my young tow-headed friend, approached from behind and startled me.

"Sure," I answered, thinking that Joey Paul and Wolfie would notice me dancing.

Showing off my best moves, I whirled and twirled to the music as my long, dusty blond hair swayed back and forth. When I peeked over my shoulder to see if Joey Paul was watching, he was gone.

Earlier, I had smelled alcohol. Then, two male skinny

dippers cannonballed into the pool. Maybe Joey Paul left because the party was too wild.

My eyes darted around the patio and settled on a group of out-of-town guys who stared at me unabashedly while munching on subs and chips.

If only I had gone home early, or never came…

"You look great in that yellow bikini. It's too bad you're too old for me." Gary laughed.

"I'm only two years older." I teased my fifteen-year old sidekick who hung out with Carly and me a lot.

Carly was closer to his age, but according to Gary, her fascination with a boy at military school killed it for him. "She talks about him constantly. Francis this… and Francis that," he had mocked one day.

After the song ended, I was determined to have fun, even though Joey Paul had chosen to leave. I held Gary's hand and we plunged into the pool. Splashing and thrashing, my young friend and I joined a game of Marco Polo with our schoolmates. Of course, the guys loved dunking the girls whenever they got a chance.

Blinking and sputtering with chlorine water in my eyes and mouth, I glanced in Wolfie's direction. Carly was in deep conversation with the handsome, Cherokee boy, and his look was still solemn… wait… Did his eyes dart my way?

If I had looked at everyone's shoes instead of their faces… I would have known…

Right in the middle of the merriment, Charlie yelled, "Quick, everybody outta here! My parents are coming up the driveway!"

Everyone scampered out of the pool, grabbed their clothes, and dashed out the screen door into the woods. Giggling and bumping into each other, we managed to escape before Mr. and Mrs. Quinn entered the house and found out about their younger son's mischief.

Poor Charlie would have been in big trouble. It was a good thing he told us to walk over or park our cars out of sight, just in case.

My memories ended abruptly when I tripped over a fallen branch and nearly landed in a briar patch. Twisting and rolling to a bare spot, I saved my skin from more cuts, but my heart raced and my breath came in short bursts.

Had I gone the wrong way? Nothing looked familiar; the trees were thicker; the sun had risen high in the sky and erased my easterly guide.

I gripped my cell phone and texted Carly, but my message wouldn't send. "Rats!" Maybe if I speed-dial... "No service. Darn it!"

Normally, little annoyances didn't bother me, but this time dread spread throughout my body. The crappy phone didn't work in the woods, and I didn't know which way to turn. If I couldn't figure this out, my parents would soon realize I was missing.

My stomach flip flopped.

Time crept by... still no houses. The hilly terrain rolled up and down, and the late afternoon sun pushed more alarm buttons. Would I have to spend another night under these cold, unsympathetic trees? Was this my punishment for not asking permission to go to the party?

Silent tears washed down my cheeks.

Suddenly, I heard crunching noises like footsteps on dried leaves. I shivered and thought of the bears and mountain lions that roamed these woods. Crouching close to a big oak tree, I listened.

A faint, melodic voice whispered on the wind that whistled through tender spring leaves. "U-wa-du-hi… a-ge-yu-tsa… a-tlo-ya-s-di. U-yo-i."

I looked up and saw a majestic eagle gliding high above the treetops. It circled as if guarding this part of the forest, and I wondered if it could see me.

At that moment, a stick cracked loudly like someone or something was close by.

Reeling around, I came face to face with an old man dressed in tattered leather clothing. He held a huge cat in his arms, and the man's wrinkled skin reminded me of the dried-apple dolls I'd seen at craft shows. In contrast, the cat's grey-striped fur was smooth and luxurious like my great aunt's mink coat. A sweet smell of cinnamon surrounded the pair, and somehow, the aroma calmed me.

"U-le-nah-i-da?" As if he were curious, the old man tilted his head when he looked at me.

Surely, he was from Qualla Boundary. I recognized the sound of the Cherokee language, but I had no idea what he said.

Was I on Cherokee land?

Some called it a *reservation*, but my teacher said the Cherokee Nation purchased 57,000 acres of this mountainous territory in the 1800's, and the title was held in a federal trust. Other American Indian tribes lived on reservations through treaties with the United States government.

This part of North Carolina was saturated with Cherokee history. The local Cherokee museums, the live re-enactment plays, and the Cherokee casino/resort brought tourism trade to the area every year.

So, why hadn't I learned any Cherokee words?

Hopefully, the man knows my language and will help me find my way home.

Chapter Two – Saved

"Can… you… speak… English?" I pronounced my words slowly and gestured with my hands.

With his head held sideways, he stared at me, sniffed the air, and crinkled his nose. After a moment's hesitation, he answered, "A little."

"You've got to help me." With overpowering emotion, my bottom lip quivered. "I'm lost!"

"I know." His kind eyes studied me from head to toe. "U-dv-hi-s-di."

"I don't know what that means. Please, point me in the direction of the closest houses, stores, anything… so I can call my friends," I pleaded.

"We go up there." He pointed his forefinger toward the nearest slope and gently placed the furry, big-eared cat on the ground.

That's the wrong way, I thought. Hadn't I just come from there?

"Come." He motioned.

"No, I have to go home. You don't understand. Last night, I fell and was knocked unconscious for hours."

"E-he-na."

The old Cherokee's worn leather moccasins stepped farther and farther away. He wasn't giving me a choice.

With teary eyes, I watched the cat, its fluffy tail pointing straight up, as it trotted behind the man.

"Wait! Don't leave me!"

The enormous feline turned its fur-collared neck toward me, grinning, it seemed… and beckoned me with its jewel-green eyes.

With no other option, I followed them up and down the rocky ground until we came to a cliff that overlooked a waterway. It was the Oconaluftee River, a river sacred to the Cherokee Nation.

I had heard stories of bears feeding on fish in the river and nervously looked around for any signs of animal life. Regardless of the danger, I knew the rolling stream would lead me to civilization, and I was grateful.

Looking at the man, I spoke cordially. "My name's Nikki. What's yours?"

He gazed at me blankly before he spoke. "Ni-ki, you call me A-do-nv-do Ga-na-tla-i."

I giggled. "That's too long."

"Okay… my name Ka-i-e-le A-da-we-hi."

"No, that's still too long… something shorter."

He flashed his yellowed teeth for the first time. "Call me A-da-we-hi."

"That's better. And what's your cat's name?"

Adawehi twisted his mouth from side to side and thought for a second like he just made up the name. "Ki-mi We-sa."

"So, tell me, which direction should I go?" I smiled at my rescuers.

"Ni-ki, you follow river… one mile… see casino." He waved his arm to the left.

"Thank you, thank you, but aren't you coming with me?"

"I see you again at Ka-ga-li, the Bony Moon…" He paused. "Maybe… Snowy Moon, too." Nodding his head in the affirmative, he began walking the opposite way.

"What does that mean?" I called after him, but he didn't stop and neither did Kimi Wesa.

Glancing toward the river, I checked to see if I could cross the terrain. When I turned back, Adawehi had vanished into a thicket of creeping kudzu vines.

The soft whispering sound whistled above me again, and I watched the eagle circle once then zoom out of sight. My confidence was renewed, and I started walking toward civilization.

Climbing down the embankment, I trudged cautiously along the stony river bank. With one eye on the lookout for bears, I sucked on honeysuckle blooms to sustain my energy. No animals were in sight, so I dipped my fingers into the cool, fresh water of the Oconaluftee and drank out of cupped hands.

After washing my face and cleaning the wound on my head, I felt much better and continued my trek.

As the sun was setting, a hazy view of the casino peeked through the never-ending trees like a beacon of light. Tears of joy trickled down my chapped cheeks, and I was happy to be alive.

Overwhelmed with gratitude, I shouted into the woods, "Thank you, Adawehi, for leading me out of the forest! Thank you, God, for the sun that woke me this morning, for the moon I see peeking over the mountain, and for the Cherokee casino!"

Half running and half stumbling, I staggered toward the huge resort in the heavy grayness of sundown.

Right away, my phone dinged with text messages and showed twelve missed calls, but I ignored them. I called Carly, and in minutes, she had picked me up in her yellow, open-air jeep. I could have walked home to the Foothills Estates, two miles away, but I was exhausted and still hoped to arrive before mom and dad.

Plopping onto the jeep's cracked seat cushion, I finally felt safe. Unfortunately, my joy didn't last long.

"Where have you been? Your parents called the police and all your friends… and they know about the pool party. Why didn't you answer your phone or message someone?" Carly sounded concerned and annoyed at the same time.

My stomach sank to the floor. Probably, Dad was pissed, and mom was frantic. My plan to get home first didn't work out. *Now what?*

"My cell phone was out of a service area." I replied to her last question only.

"What did you tell my parents?" My heart beat rapidly, and I experienced a different kind of panic.

"That I hadn't seen you since Friday night, of course." Carly paused. "Well… what happened? Where were you?"

My mind was spinning. How would my parents react when they heard my explanation? It didn't even sound believable to me.

Our house was only one house away from Charlie's, and all the neighborhood kids grew up playing Hide and Seek, Simon Says, and Scavenger Hunt in the trees. Our moms signaled lunch or dinner time by ringing a bell.

Frequently, my mom would call us in for cookies, popsicles, or lemonade and tell me to keep the house within sight. *Did she think I might get lost then? Will she believe me now?*

She had always kept the peace and defended me and my

brother when we got into trouble. Dad, on the other hand, was more distrustful.

Not long ago, he accused me of denting my car, but mom proved an animal had run into *me* by finding deer hair in the dent.

I glanced at Carly and saw suspicion on her face... even before I said anything.

"Did you spend the night with a boy?" She smirked.

"No, of course not! When we ran out of the party, I fell into a ravine and hit my head. I woke up this morning and got turned around. An old Cherokee man helped me find the casino."

"Right," she said, sarcastically. "Is that the story you want me to spread?"

"It's not a story! It's the truth!" I was aggravated that my best friend didn't believe me.

Sitting in silence the rest of the way home, I tried not to breathe in the exhaust fumes from Saturday night's traffic.

As soon as Carly drove up my winding driveway, I jumped out of the bouncy jeep. With a brusque "Thank you," I rushed past pots of pink geraniums, stormed into the house, and slammed the front door.

Bolting up to my room, I shut the door and dove face-down into the duvet coverlet. I had done nothing wrong, except for going to an unchaperoned party.

My best friend thought I did something shameful. *Is that what my parents will think?*

"Nikki? Nikki is that you?" My mother yelled from downstairs with uneasiness in her voice.

"Boy, are you in for it." Bogey chuckled as he cracked open my door.

"Get out!" I screamed.

Mom barged past Bogey and sat down on the bed. "Are you okay? Are you hurt?" She stroked my tangled hair. "Your dad and I were worried sick until Carly phoned and said she was bringing you home. What happened?"

"I'm fine. Nothing happened. I just need to sleep." I hoped she would leave. "May I please tell you about it tomorrow?"

"Your father wants to see you tonight, downstairs, in the kitchen. He knows you went to Charlie Quinn's party..." Mom continued to chat like she was giving my father time to cool off.

"...last night's rain storm cancelled his trail ride, and when I returned this afternoon, I suspected you hadn't been home..." She paused, perhaps to give me time to comment, but I was too tired.

"You didn't answer your phone, so we called friends and were told the police had investigated a loud party on Friday evening at the Quinn's. At that point, we panicked and reported you missing..."

Poor Charlie. His parents found out anyway.

When mom finished talking, I breathed deeply and squared my shoulders. "Okay, I'm ready to talk to him." My eyelids quivered with apprehension.

The grilling wasn't as bad as I had imagined. I told the truth as I knew it. Nonetheless, he grounded me for the whole summer. He said I "snuck off" to the party and lied about where I'd been all night. *But I didn't lie!*

"Did you go off with a boy?" he demanded.

"No!" I stomped my foot.

I thought mom believed me, but I was past caring.

Sprinting up the stairs, I jumped into a steamy shower

and fell into bed without eating the sandwich she had fixed. I felt sick.

Waking early the next morning, I thought yesterday had been a bad dream. However, my aching bones and the stinging cut above my eye brought me back to reality.

Mom rapped softly on the door and brought in my breakfast.

"Here's your favorite, oatmeal with blueberries. Let me see that cut again. You may need stitches."

"No, it's okay." I pulled away.

"Do you want to discuss what happened?" She leaned in and tucked a wayward strand of hair behind my ear.

"Mom, I'm telling the truth. I fell and hit my head. End of story!" I dug into the warm oats like a person who only had honeysuckle and a few blackberries the day before.

"And the Cherokee was... an *old* man, not a young man?" she quizzed.

I stopped eating and gazed out the window at the bird house dad had built when I was a little girl. He said cardinals would love being high in the chestnut tree away from neighborhood cats. I miss those early years and... that dad.

"Honey, I just want to make sure you're... not... in trouble. You can tell me anything." Ever since a girl in my school got pregnant, my parents often brought up the topic of sex.

Even if they didn't believe it, I knew I'd never sleep with a boy unless we loved each other and got married. But me, married? I didn't think so. I wanted a degree in Art History or something... to get away from these mountains... to be a professor in a neat college somewhere... to travel to Europe... maybe Italy. *Dr. Nikki Loveleigh.*

Yet, why did I keep thinking about Joey Paul and now Wolfie?

"Mom, I'm telling you exactly what happened. I'm sorry I went to the party without permission, but that's all I did wrong, honest!"

The days passed slowly. I spent my grounded time looking at stuff on You Tube and social media or reading books. I read about female heroines like Zena in *Sofia's Secret*. She travels to Italy, finds an ancient treasure, and saves African lions from extinction. *I need a worthwhile project.*

I yearned for adventure and wanted to be the girl in that book, anything but stuck in this house. Lounging in a chaise by the pool got old, and my tan was dark enough for a fair-skinned person.

One day, my sympathetic mother provided relief by challenging me to a game of tennis, the only sport at which I was fairly good. Leaving the house was a saving grace. I thought of my future... tennis pro... athletic coach, maybe... something active.

I hoped we would play again, but mom was busy with volunteer work. So, I endured more days of reading in the sun, humped over the computer, and parked in front of the TV.

Carly and I hadn't spoken since the night she picked me up at the casino. I supposed she had a right to question me. My pursuit of Joey Paul probably made me look boy crazy.

And none of my side-kick friends had called or texted, not Sammie, Charlie, nor Gary. What had Carly told them?

Why do I feel so bloated?

Chapter Three – Saved Again

June 8
Present Day

Brooding over memories of the last week, I nearly jump out of my skin when the house phone rings. My best friends always call or text on my cell phone, so I don't answer.

"It's for you!" Bogey yells from downstairs.

"Nikki? What's going on? Are you okay?" The sophisticated, low-pitched voice of Laura Acres, who prefers to be called Laurie, resonates with concern.

Level-headed Laura, the voice of reason, the voice of maturity, always smiles broadly like that old-time movie star, Lauren Bacall, like a person who knows all of your business. Still, I trust her opinion.

Laura, the daughter of my mother's best friend, heads the list of my second circle of friends. We don't hang out at school, but we sometimes do homework together or talk, since we're neighbors. My first circle includes Carly, or *did* include Carly.

"Why? What do you mean?" Wondering what she knows, I throw questions right back at her.

"I heard you got into big trouble after Charlie Quinn's

party, and your dad grounded you for the entire summer. Lucky for me, I decided not to go to that one."

"Bogey! Hang up the phone!" I yell at my brother through the receiver. He's a good kid but a pain in my butt.

"I'm sorry, Laurie. Can you come over, please?"

She arrives quickly from across the street where her family's home sits in a maze of trees on the hill.

After locking my door, I pour out my heart, and Laura stays all afternoon. Amazingly, she believes everything I say, even the part about the Cherokee man and the cat.

"Laurie, I'm puzzled by something Adawehi said. You volunteer on Cherokee land… What's a Bony Moon or a Snowy Moon?"

"The Cherokee call February the Bony Moon month and December the Snowy Moon month." Laura frowns like she's questioning why the man mentioned those months.

"He said he would see me then. I don't know what it means." Shaking my head, I stare at the floral scatter rug that mom handmade for my hardwood floor.

"Listen, Nikki, you need to get involved with something. Moping around here will drive you nuts." The voice of reason speaks. "I'll ask my mother if you can help with Cherokee Vacation Bible School. She's in charge of organizing the junior counselors." Laura lifts her eyebrows, nods, and beams with enthusiasm at her idea.

"For three weeks, little kids sing, paint pictures, play games and make scenery for a play about a historical American Indian event." Her voice raises, and she gestures with her hands.

But I fail to share her excitement.

"I don't get along that well with kids. The only thing my

little brother enjoys is torturing me." Sadly, I doodle on a piece of paper and draw a stick figure behind bars.

"Stop it! You're going tomorrow. It's the first day of training for the teen helpers. I guarantee you'll like the little kids, and they'll like you. Your father can't possibly object to volunteer work!" Flashing her broad, all-knowing smile, Laura hugs me good bye.

When my mother comes home from shopping, the enticing aroma of a homecooked dinner wafts up the stairs. No one can beat her vegetable lasagna, my favorite comfort food.

Soon, she calls to me. "Nikki, come down and make the salad."

I tear buttery Boston lettuce into a bowl, toss in sliced cucumbers, plop cherry tomatoes on top, and stir in a light dressing. Mom, Bogey, and I eat together.

Dad lumbers in from the barn an hour later. He sits down with us only on special occasions, or when his mother, my grandmother Bertie, comes to visit, or if we go to her house.

After supper, mom comes into my room. "Mrs. Acres wants you to volunteer at Green Hill Church for their vacation bible school for Cherokee children."

"I don't want to." I look down at the floor.

"Your father said it's a good idea for you to see what it's like to take care of a child."

My head shoots up and my eyes fill with fire. "Fine! I'll do it!"

Anything to get away from people who don't trust me.

* * * *

Tuesday morning, Mrs. Acres drives us to the picturesque

white-steeple church on the edge of Qualla Boundary, home-
land of the eastern Cherokee Indians.

Laura and I go through orientation with the other teen
counselors, some Cherokee and some not. I don't know any
of them, but they're all friendly, male and female.

Afterward, we learn to make dreamcatchers for the children who will start next week. The constructed example
is circular with webby-looking string inside and with dan-
gly-stuff attached. I've seen lots of them in gift shops but
never tried to put one together.

According to an American Indian legend if you hang a
dreamcatcher above your bed, it will keep bad dreams out
and let good dreams in.

In my first attempt, I bend willow-wood into a hoop and
weave a tangled web of green yarn through it. To the wooden
ring, I fasten uneven strips of black leather, tie on gray
chicken feathers, sew on purple beads, and then grimace at
the muddled mess. It would surely scare away nightmares.
Ha!

Laura skillfully interlaces a dreamcatcher with yellow
yarn and uses white feathers and alternating red and blue
beads to accent her creation. It reminds me of the red, blue,
and yellow corn that grows neatly in grandpa Loveleigh's
rowed field.

Every fall, I look forward to grandpa's corn-shucking
parties. Whoever finds a red or blue ear of corn first, wins
a prize.

After my friend and I giggle at my lack of craft skills, I
thank her for saving me from self-pity and boredom. Vacation bible school may be fun after all.

Knock, knock, knock!

A loud pounding startles everyone, and we watch as Mrs. Acres opens the door.

"You're late, but come in. We can always use another set of hands."

A Cherokee boy walks into the room, and I glance at Laura with a nervous blink.

"Wow! Who is he?" Laura's green eyes pop when she sees him.

Not looking in his direction, I lower my head and whisper. "That's Wolfie. He came to Charlie's pool party."

Should I say "Hi" or pretend I don't know him?

Just as I decide to acknowledge him, one of the ladies introduces Wolfie Romano.

Wolfie singles me out from the rest and stares. When he speaks in Cherokee, his almost-too-white teeth break through his smooth, coppery lips. "A-si-yu, Nikki Loveleigh."

I'm stunned. How does he know my name?

"What did he say?" I question Laura as quietly as I can.

"I said, '*Hello*, Nikki Loveleigh.'" A playful smirk cuts across his bronze face.

I nod my greeting and turn away.

Embarrassed that I don't even know how to say "hello" in Cherokee, I grab a hoop and start weaving pink yarn. This time, I challenge myself to make a pretty dreamcatcher.

Mrs. Acres assigns Wolfie the job of organizing props for the children's historical play, "Trail of Tears."

In the 1830's, President Andrew Jackson approved the Indian Removal Act that forced many tribes to leave their homes in the southeast and walk long distances to reservations west of the Mississippi river. Thousands of Cherokee natives died on the last walk in 1838, truly a trail of tears for the families who were broken apart and lost loved ones. The few who remained in North Carolina grew in numbers and populate today's Qualla Boundary.

The adult counselors at Green Hill Church teach the Cherokee children about Christianity, but they believe it's important for them to learn about their own culture and heritage, too.

While working on my dreamcatcher, I peeked discreetly at Wolfie's sandals. Of course, he can't be wearing *the* black sneakers, since I saw one shoe in the woods.

Laura catches me glancing at him and snickers. "What happened to Joey Paul?"

It seems everyone at school knows I'm in love with Joey Paul. "Stop it!" I command, playfully.

Lunchtime rolls around, and the junior counselors grab a boxed lunch provided by the church. We sit outside on the grass, and Wolfie parks himself on the other side of Laura.

I lean over to look him in the eye and rudely blurt my words. "How do you know my name, and why is your name Wolfie?"

"I asked Charlie about you." He pauses, then answers my second question.

"Cherokee mothers choose strong names for their sons. Mine named me Wolfman… and… my last name is Romano because my father is Italian."

"Oh." I respond, sheepishly, and don't ask anymore questions.

Wolfie seems mysterious. Every time I catch him gazing at me, he quickly turns away. Does he like me, or is he shy, or is he just sizing me up like a… like a… wolf?

I've never had a steady boyfriend like most of my girl-friends. Prettier girls live in this town, yet people admire my thick, blond hair, blue-green eyes, and tall, thin frame.

The day ends quickly, and I find myself looking forward to tomorrow, but…

My breakfast won't stay down, and I don't feel well at all. Mom says I picked up a stomach virus. So, without me, Laura and her mom drive to the little church and report back that Wolfie Romano asked where I was. *Really?*

Thursday is boring. Wolfie isn't there, but work continues on the scenery, props, and costumes for the play.

On Friday, the adults meet with the teens and give instructions for the official start of vacation bible school next week. Wolfie mopes through his assignments and doesn't speak all day. I feel dumb for thinking he would be glad to see me.

I spend Saturday at home alone. Carly calls in the evening and chats like everything is normal. She tells me about her trip to Lake Tahoe and hiking on the rocky trails, which turn into ski runs in the wintertime.

We establish that she's not mad and I'm not mad. When she hears that I'm grounded, she lightheartedly suggests that we meet at Horse Chips, a sandwich shop and favorite teenage hangout.

After pondering her rebellious idea for a second, I agree. Leaving the house shouldn't be difficult. Dad's trail ride meeting will occupy him, and mom's bridge club meets across town.

I crank up my old, blue corvette, roll down the white convertible top, rumble down our twisty driveway, and cruise Highway 19 to the designated place. When I pull up next to Carly's jeep, some of the guys from Charlie's party hoot and holler. With not much to do in small towns, teens gather in restaurant parking lots, or in fields near a lake, or a river.

Delighting in my freedom, I turn off the roar of the eight-cylinder engine and shake my hair loose. Even the greasy smell of burgers and fries wafting through the air doesn't bother me.

Carly jumps into my car. "You'll never guess who's here?"

"Joey Paul?" My anticipation mounts.

"Wolfie! You know, from the party… I heard that he and his girlfriend broke up." Carly enjoys catching me up on the latest gossip.

"Oh… where is he?" I don't tell her that I've seen Wolfie at Green Hill Church.

Carly motions toward the purple Charger beside her jeep. I wave to get his attention, but either he ignores the gesture or he is blind.

Filled with guys, the car sways with music and laughter. Charlie, Sammie, and Gary sit in the back. Wolfie and an unknown boy are in the front. On the other side of the Charger, a red Mustang rocks with football jocks who strain to get a glimpse of Carly and me. I guess we're the only girls here so far.

With his red hair gleaming from the light of a nearby neon sign, my friend Charlie rests his arms on the purple car's window frame.

"Tsk, tsk, tsk." He admonishes me for I-don't-know-what and then shakes his head in disbelief.

"What's he doing?" I question Carly.

"Oh, you know. Boys talk."

"No, I don't know. Talk about what?" I demand.

"Who was it?" She smiles slyly. "Who was with you in the woods?"

"What? This is too much. Get out!" I shout at Carly. "You're my best friend and you don't believe me!" My eyelids flutter.

Speeding home, I'm so pissed that I pass a car on the hill and almost collide with an oncoming bus. Luckily, mom and dad haven't returned, and Bogey has spent the night with a friend, so no one hears my tires squeal up the driveway.

But, wait… is that a large gray cat sitting in our mimosa tree? When I blink to clear my teary eyes, it isn't there.

Sunday morning, I pretend to be sick, although I *really* don't feel well. Mom attends church, and dad works in his office at the barn. Carly texts an apology, and Laura calls to remind me of the official start of vacation bible school on Monday.

* * * *

Giggling, singing, drawing, and dancing, the children bop through their first day, and their joy fills my heart. Laura and I help supervise the activities inside, and Wolfman Romano oversees the playground outside. As someone once said, "Out of sight, out of mind."

The week flies by and not a word from Wolfie. Who cares. Who needs a boyfriend? I'm never getting married anyway.

Laura and I work well together until…

Friday, lunchtime: She puts her sandwich down and gazes at me. "My friend Eddie says the boys in town are saying things about you."

"What things? What do you mean, Laurie?"

"About the night of Charlie's party… when you were in the woods… that you and a boy were… you know." She grins like she ate the last cookie on the plate.

"No, I *don't* know!" I scream. "I told you exactly what happened. Why would they say that?"

Fortunately, I have my car today, so I excuse myself from the closing activities and speed home with tears flowing, again.

Who was talking about me? What actually happened in that ravine?

Chapter Four – Panic

No one calls or texts all weekend, and neither reading nor sunbathing does much to cheer me.

Dragging myself to get dressed for another week at Green Hill Church, I suddenly remember to pack some tampons in my purse. My last cycle ended 28 days ago. How embarrassing it would be to have an accident.

Laura doesn't say much today, and Wolfie's quiet manner suits me just fine.

The kids laugh, play, and sing the day away, ending my sullen mood. Some of the children wear worn-out clothes and hand-me-down moccasins, but they still bubble with delight.

Watching the little ones, I'm filled with a desire to help them escape the poverty created by a lack of educational opportunities. The young people marry and have more babies; it's a tough cycle to break. Half of the funds from the Indian casino is divided among full tribal adult members, but it doesn't amount to a lot.

Working with the Cherokee children has opened my eyes to the problems of tribal life. Up until now, my head has been buried in my own self-centered life.

Aponi, a barefooted little five-year-old, steals my heart. Her name means butterfly, and it fits her. She flits from friend to friend spreading her joy. Aponi sings to one, then twirls for another, and then helps a younger child with a project.

While I'm observing her, an "aha" moment strikes. Instead of saving lions like the girl in "Sofia's Secret," a heartfelt goal for me would be improving the quality of life for American Indian kids.

In my head, I devise a plan. I'll major in American Indian studies, learn to speak their languages, and devote my life to educating the children. With more knowledge, they'll have the power to attain better jobs.

"Nikki?"

Startled, my daydream vanishes, and I stare into Wolfie's handsome face. Part Italian, part American Indian, his perfect Roman nose nestles neatly between his chiseled cheekbones.

"What?" Gathering my composure, I manage to answer him.

"Sorry I've been avoiding you." He hangs his head. "It's just that... well, you know the guys were passing around tequila at Charlie's party... and some of them teased me for... liking you." His face contorts into a frown.

Not having seen this side of Wolfie, I gaze at him and try to decide what's in his heart. It takes a minute to comprehend what he said.

"Wait... You like me?" I pause, lost for words other than the obvious. "Why?"

At that moment, two little girls dance around us and chant, "U-wa-du-hi... a-ge-yu-tsa... a-da-ga-u-e... wa-ya-i!"

"No, I don't think so." Wolfie's white toothy smile returns.

"What did they say?"

"You don't want to know."

"I hate this. Tell me!" I demand, stomping my foot.

"You need to learn Cherokee for yourself." He walks away.

All-knowing Laura looks up from her group of six-year-old's and chuckles.

"They said, 'Pretty girl loves Wolfie.'"

"Why would they say that?" My face blushes fiery pink.

Shaking my head and rolling my eyes, I turn away and dig into a box of acrylic paints. I find a large jar of verde green and enlist three of the older kids to paint an oak tree on the canvas backdrop for the play.

Pondering Wolfie's words, my eyes light up. Do I like him more than Joey Paul? I don't know. Maybe Wolfie and I can work together to help American Indian children.

Leaving the children to paint, I search for Wolfie on the playground and find him coaching young soccer players.

I motion him to the sidelines. "Do you own a pair of black, high-top tennis shoes?"

"Every guy owns a pair of black sneakers." He squints and stares at me in a weird way.

"But have you lost one shoe?"

"I… don't… think so." Averting his eyes, he shakes his head, negatively.

Rats! I'll never figure this out.

That night, in my mind, I replay the conversation with Wolfman Romano.

Why do the other boys tease him for liking me? Has he heard the stories that Carly and Laura heard?

Whose footprints were in the ravine? Did more than one person fall with me? Why hasn't my period started?

****

Days go by and still no flow. Since mom does all the laundry, she questions me. I assure her my tummy is bloated and it will happen soon. But it doesn't.

One afternoon, Laura reminds me of the July 4th picnic and fireworks by Lake Junaluska, but honestly, I don't feel like it, even if dad would consent. Instead, I lie on my bed and listen to local pops, bangs, and hissing noises until I fall asleep around midnight.

Another week begins, and mom insists on taking me to our doctor who orders lots of tests.

When the results come back, I scream. I cry. My mother cries. How can I be **pregnant**?! It doesn't make any sense. I've done nothing wrong. I'm a virgin!

The footprints! Someone attacked me in that ravine and left me for dead!

"Please, don't tell dad." I plead with mom, but she promises only to wait until she's in a calmer state of mind.

In desperation, I confide in Laura. Maybe she can say or do something to help me sort this out. Wrong! She promptly blabs to her mother.

Immediately, Mrs. Acres tells my dad who already suspects I was with a boy in the woods, which I wasn't.

Mr. Vern Loveleigh blows his top; Mrs. Alise Loveleigh throws up.

I quit the last week of Cherokee Vacation Bible School. My stomach feels huge, and I can't face Laura, the kids, or Wolfie. *What will he think of me now?*

For the first two days, my father yells obscenities every time he looks at me; my mother continues to sob, and I shrink into nothingness.

While I wallow in confusion and self-pity, a memory of the old Indian man pops into my head. Grabbing my new Cherokee dictionary, I hold my breath and tremble as Adawehi's words ring in my ears. He said "U-dv-hi-s-di" as soon as we met. Flipping through the pages, I find the meaning... fertile. Fertile?

He knew. Adawehi knew then. But how?

Looking up his name, I am stunned. My jaw drops and my eyes pop when the word "angel" jumps out at me.

Adawehi is an angel! He led me out of the forest. He saved me.

Burying my head in the bed pillow, I cry myself to sleep.

Early the next morning before anyone else wakes up, I escape into the woods. I want my angel to find me again... maybe he can fix this.

Feverishly, I dodge drooping magnolia branches and white oak saplings. For more than an hour, I sprint over rocks and logs, climb up hilly terrain, and scramble toward the last place I saw Adawehi, at the river. With labored breath, I arrive at a cliff above the Oconaluftee. Hypnotized by the rapid waters, I'm conscious of only one thing: I don't want to live, not like this.

Wilting like a hibiscus bloom that survives only one day, my body rolls down, down to the river's babbling border. Dirt and leaf debris stick to my skin, and pebbles and stones indent my face and hands.

When I crash into the cold abyss, an innate will to live awakens. Instinctively, I thrash my arms and legs and fight the river's determination. Bobbing up and down in the fast-moving current, I see my short life flash in front of me. Do I want to die so soon? Do I really want to kill the being inside of me?

Then, a soft whisper, barely audible above the white-water noise, fills my senses. My angel calls me from afar.

"Ni-ki, e-he-na. Ni-ki, e-he-na. Ni-ki, e-he-na."

Clearer and louder now, the welcome sound dominates the river's growl, and its liquid death pools into a calm cove. Clawing my way to the edge, my fingernails dig into the rich mud that teems with crawdads, earthworms, and other tiny creatures.

I drag my dripping body up the embankment, through patches of green ferns, past wriggly insects, chirping crickets, and hard-shelled bugs. Something or someone nudges me forward.

Lifting my eyes to the sky, I blink several times and focus on a bald eagle that soars far above the treetops. *Is it the same eagle I saw before?*

"On the Wings of an Eagle," plays in my mind, and my crawl quickens.

I grab a small tree branch to pull myself upright, and I'm surprised to see a petite dogwood in full bloom at the top of the bluff. Noticing the white blossoms shaped like little crosses, I remember a legendary story.

In biblical times in Jerusalem, the crucifixion crosses were made out of dogwood trees that were huge and towered over other trees. After Jesus was crucified, God dwarfed the tree so the dogwood would never grow large enough for that purpose again.

The brown puncture mark on each petal of the bloom symbolizes the nail scar from Jesus's hands and feet. The blossom's beaded center represents the crown of thorns placed on His head…

Staring at the river below, the little tree supports me while I consider my near-death experience. In spite of being soaking wet, I decide to follow the angel's voice and trudge deeper into the forest.

Glimpsing movement in the undergrowth ahead, I imagine Kimi Wesa, the gray tabby cat, trotting in front of me on this somewhat-familiar path.

Adawehi's melodious words, quieter now, calm me as I walk. I must find him; I must have answers.

The noonday sun shines through the army of hardwoods, casts playful patterns on the woodland's vegetation, and warms my dampened soul. Lingering to inhale the earthy smells of green moss and musky tree bark, I spot tiny ants scurrying along a wilderness trail. A closer look reveals miniature wildflowers of lavender, yellow, and blue peeping around wild grass for their share of the sun. In this peaceful place, I'm almost able to forget my troubles. Almost.

The elfish white dogwood and flowering redbud trees mark an easy pathway through the tall woods of birch and hickory. Surely, this is the same trail Adawehi used, except I don't remember blooming trees.

Why did these springtime trees bloom in July? Did Adawehi do this to guide me?

Suddenly, out of a clear sky, a distant rumbling gets my attention. I glance up at the blue heavens then back to the ground and notice a deep ravine just ahead.

It's the gully I fell into when I ran from the pool party. Questioning my sanity for returning here, I inch down the steep-sided gulch.

Parting the chokeberry and barberry bushes that fill this canyon-like gorge, I find the black tennis shoe lying on the trampled ground.

To my surprise, the most stunning flower grows next to the despised footwear. Dappled with red, yellow, and blue, the colorful bloom reminds me of a large lollipop, and its crinkly, dark green foliage resembles the mature spinach leaves in mother's garden.

The unfurled blossom displays the double petals of a peony, the flute of a daffodil, and the bearded center of an iris. I am mesmerized by its beauty, and not noticing the protruding thorns, I attempt to pluck it from this hostile ground.

"Ouch!"

The prickly protrusions warn onlookers not to touch nature's creation, and a tiny droplet of blood forms on my index finger.

"A-do-nv-do Ad-si-la. A-do-nv-do Ad-si-la."

My attention turns away from my wound when I hear the haunting voice of Adawehi.

Breathing in the delightful scent of raw cinnamon, I sense his spirit all around me. Patiently, I sit down on dry leaves and wait for Adawehi to appear.

As the musical chant fades and the aroma diminishes, I realize the angel's presence will not be physical this time.

Stillness hangs over the silent forest, yet the perfect blossom sways as if Adawehi's essence stirs the air when he leaves.

The light of day dwindles, and I yearn for the comfort of my own bed. Climbing up the slope of the ravine, I glance back at the lollipop flower and watch the petals furl tightly together in anticipation of a cooler night.

Backtracking the mystical route marked by the blossoming dogwood and redbud trees, I repeat Adawehi's words until I'm out of the forest.

My Cherokee dictionary will reveal his message.

Chapter Five – The Plan

At home, mom cooks shrimp and grits, and my empty stomach rumbles.

Dad lingers at the barn as usual, so mom, Bogey, and I sit down to eat in peace and quiet.

I try to catch a glance from my mother. I want to smile at her, to show her I'm happy to be alive, but she avoids my gaze through the whole meal.

Does my mother hate me for being pregnant?

My brother picks at his plate and raises his head only once or twice like he's waiting for an impending storm. I think he understands the gravity of my situation.

After the dishes are done, I retreat to my room and grab the Cherokee dictionary. Turning to the A's, I find a-do-nv-do. It means spirit. Okay…. Running my finger down the page, I find ad-sil-la… blossom. Spirit blossom? Why would the angel whisper "spirit blossom"?

Was he calling the lollipop flower a spirit blossom?

Confused, I sit still and listen for my inner voice, and the answer rushes into my head. Adawehi has named the *baby*! There, I can say it… baby. Baby, baby, baby.

Muffling sobs into my pillow, I still can't believe I'm pregnant.

Maybe the doctor read someone else's test, or maybe the results were wrong.

Nausea overtakes me and tonight's shrimp and grits fly into the toilet.

"Nikki? Nikki?" My father's harsh, unforgiving voice erupts into my room.

"Yes?" I wipe my mouth as I exit the bathroom.

"Where were you today? With that boy, again?"

"Dad, I was not with a boy, and I haven't ever *been* with a boy! I just went for a walk." I ball my hands into fists.

"So, what? Are you pregnant with nobody's baby? In the morning, your mother will make an appointment for an abortion. This will end once and for all… and don't forget you are grounded!" he barks.

Blotches of red, blue, and purple cover my father's face like he's turning into a Dr. Jekyll-Mr. Hyde personality. He regards me with scorn, with eyes I don't recognize.

Some senseless boy has done this to my family? How can we go on living normal lives after he raped me?

My head swims with thoughts and questions. Adawehi wants me to keep the baby. Otherwise, why would he name it?

Kids should listen to their parents, right? But mom hasn't spoken out. What does she really think about an abortion?

"Dad, please don't hate me. I didn't do what you think. I hit my head, and someone must've attacked me when I was unconscious." As I speak, I recall the terrifying nightmare before I awoke in the woods.

Is it possible the dream reflected what was happening to me?

"Right," he says, sarcastically. Storming out of the room, he looks back over his shoulder. "Get rid of it!"

I hold onto my dictionary like a security blanket and look up more words... kimi... wesa... secret cat?

Who names a cat Secret Cat?

Exhausted, I plop onto my bed, and all emotion drains out of my body. Pulling soft bedcovers up to my chin, I stare at my best dreamcatcher dangling from the headboard.

Please, let only the good dreams come through...

Squinting at daybreak, I dare to hope this whole pregnancy thing is a night terror that will erase from my memory. But, no... I lie in bed and remember every detail of that fateful weekend, everything except... being raped.

Bogey cracks open the door and pushes his laughing face into my room. "Breakfast for two waiting for you downstairs. Ha! Ha!"

Slamming a pillow against the door, I almost score a hit before he ducks.

At the table, mom seems lost for words. "Your father... wants me..."

"I know. He told me last night."

"Is that what you want?" Her face shows wrinkles that I haven't noticed before.

"Mom, I don't know what I want, except that I don't want to be pregnant. Not now." I tear up.

"Bogey, finish your pancakes in your room. I need to talk to Nikki."

"But, mom..."

"Now." Her stern voice gives him no choice.

After my brother leaves, my mother's eyes search mine. Waiting until she speaks first, I glance away. In my mind's eye, I see Aponi, the happy little Cherokee girl flitting around the other children at vacation bible school.

I imagine my baby is a girl, Adsila.

In my vision, a multi-colored butterfly glides down and lands on the yellow, red, and blue flower in the forest. The butterfly and the bloom blend together and form one beautiful child, my child.

How can I destroy such a sweet joy?

Abruptly, my thoughts change to a teenager trying to raise a helpless baby by herself, and it's inconceivable.

Is dad right? Is abortion the answer?

"Nikki, talk to me. What do you want to do? I'll support whatever decision you make." My mother's gentle promise confirms that she's on my side, whatever that side may be.

"Mom, how can I answer? I'm seventeen. This is the last thing I expected to happen to me. And I don't know for sure that it did happen. I don't remember anything, except…"

"Except, what?" she questions. "Tell me, it may help."

"On the night of the party, someone may have pushed me into the ravine when we ran through the woods. Accidentally, or on purpose… I don't know. It was very dark and people were bumping into each other. I fell, rolled down the slope, and hit my head. I awoke on Saturday, and my bikini was ripped. When I looked for my clothes, I saw… a shoe."

"What shoe?"

"I found a boy's black tennis shoe on top of one of my sneakers."

My mother perks up. "So, you didn't give your consent?"

"No, mom. That's what I've been telling you and dad all along." I sigh and roll my eyes.

"You were raped! And the shoe is a clue. Do you have it?" Her face lightens.

Apparently, she's happy that I didn't agree to have sex.

Does it matter? I'm still pregnant!

"No, it's still in the woods. I saw it yesterday."

"Anything else?"

"Just lots of footprints… and… I think the old man who led me out of the woods is an angel. His name means 'angel' in the Cherokee language."

Mom looks at me with doubting eyes and ignores the last half of my statement.

Why did I even mention it?

"A shoe and footprints at the scene changes everything. You shouldn't feel guilty about having an abortion. You were forced." It sounds like mom's attitude has flip flopped.

Is she in favor of an abortion now instead of being on my side?

"Mom, it doesn't change anything for me. How can I kill a baby?"

"It's not a baby yet." She avoids eye contact with me.

"That's what you say, but I know it is."

Adawehi knew that a baby was inside me. As soon as we met, he said the word "fertile" in Cherokee. Yesterday, he gave me a sign that I should *keep* the baby… a single large flower blooming in the forest… in the ravine… in the shade!"

"I'll tell your father about these new circumstances. Maybe he'll agree to delay making an appointment until we think this through." She doesn't acknowledge the word "keep."

Sprinting upstairs, I slam the door and pace the floor. The only thing on my mind is texting Laura, the voice of reason, to get her take on the blossom.

"Oh, Laurie, thank you for coming over." I hug her when

she arrives. "I was mad at you for telling your mother… but it was the right thing to do. Someone had to speak up."

"Tell me all that's happened." Her serious green eyes study me.

When I finish my story about the large flower and the Cherokee name, she gazes at me with skepticism. "So, you think the old man was an angel from heaven… and he has named the baby Spirit Blossom?"

"Yes, yes!" I affirm with a vigorous nod.

"Nikki, did you suffer a concussion when you fell in the woods?"

"No, it's true. I'll show you the flower."

"Trekking around in the forest is not my forte, but that's not the problem. You being pregnant is the *problem*." She emphasizes the last word.

"Laurie, do you remember Aponi… the delightful little barefoot girl who helped the other children at vacation bible school?"

"Of course, the butterfly." Laura smiles for the first time since arriving.

"I think of her every time my father says the word 'abortion.' How can I kill a little baby who could grow up to be like Aponi?" I sob.

Laura stares into space for a few minutes like she's weighing the situation. "This happened to you for a reason. If the old man was really an angel, and he gave you a sign with a flower and a name for the baby… then it's destiny. You cannot let anyone talk you into aborting this pregnancy." Laura's conclusion rings of finality.

Without words, we gaze at each other, and I sense she's considering the hardships of an unwed mother's future, just as I am.

"Do you have any clues that might identify the boy who did this? Maybe his family would help."

"Well, only the shoe…"

Before I finish the sentence, my father bursts into the room. "Tell me about the shoe you found!" he commands. "I'll find that rapist, and he'll wish he was dead!"

Laura and I gasp at the threat, at the alien look on my father's face, and at the menacing tone of his voice.

Dad's attitude was explosive when he thought I consented to sex, but now, realizing a crime was committed, he had completely lost control.

"Dad, I-I don't want you to hurt anyone," I stutter.

"Maybe the police could… find…" Laura pauses.

He leers at Laura. "You'd best go home now, Laura. No one else can know about this. Do you understand?"

"Adoption is another option." She glares at my father.

"Laura… home!" He growls through gritted teeth, and she backs out of my bedroom.

Shouting threats, my father paces, waves his arms, and vows to find the responsible boy.

"Where is that shoe?" His demanding tone brings out my stubborn streak.

"It's deep in the woods, but I won't show you." For the first time, I defy my father, and I feel empowered.

"Vern." My peacekeeping mother slips into the room. "Let's discuss this later, when we're calm."

His mouth curls and twitches, and for a moment, I think he's going to hit her. Instead, he vaults out the door, sprints down the stairs, and slams the back porch door.

Mom and I expel our held breath.

Stunned at my father's threats to harm someone, I sit quietly while mom hugs me. She says I don't have to rush into having an abortion... that I still have time, if I decide to do it.

She puts on a brave face, but I feel compassion for my mother. *Her only daughter... pregnant at seventeen.*

I can't remember what happened, but I know this pregnancy has turned three lives upside down. For that, I am furious! A horrible boy has done this to me and to my parents. A lustful, self-centered jerk has ruined my hopes and dreams... my life.

I'm sure that's why dad's temper exploded. His expectations for my future have vanished because of someone's impulsive, violent act.

"Mom... I..."

Oooga!

My cell phone interrupts, and I see it's Laura calling. My voice-of-reason friend says texting is impersonal.

"Don't say anything if your parents are in the room. Just listen." Laura instructs me before I can say hello. "I know a place you can go until it's too late for an abortion. Come over to my house the first chance you get."

Hanging up without a word, I feel my eye lids begin to blink, which always happens when I'm nervous.

"Who was that?" Mom looks at me curiously.

"I-I think it was a wrong number."

I hate fibbing to my mother, but I'm desperate. I don't know if I can fully trust her?

My father is trying to control me, even though I'm *almost* eighteen. Shouldn't I have a say in this? People fight in wars when they are eighteen.

That evening, I duck out the front while dad tends the horses, mom tidies the kitchen, and Bogey puzzles over his homework. Breathing heavily as I climb the Acres' steep driveway, I make a mental note. *Breathless, exercise more. Is it okay to play tennis and swim, if you're pregnant?*

Laura's parents are attending a meeting, so we're alone as she spells out her plan. She knows a family on Qualla Boundary who takes in abused kids or ones whose parents have been arrested. Laura believes they will hide me.

"Seriously? Hide from mom and dad?" I'm doubtful of her idea. However, deep down, I know the answer. Dropping out of sight would give me time to think. Time and space—two things I don't have at my house.

Laura gazes at me with her all-knowing green eyes and lifts her eyebrows, questioning.

"Okay, I agree. How? When? Where?"

"Leave the details to me. In a few days, after I contact the family, I'll call you. And this time it'll be our secret."

After leaving Laura, I don't feel like returning home. I walk and walk until I notice a well-lit church tucked away on a side street. Why haven't I seen this church before? It looks like a Catholic church, a small cathedral, like the ones in travel ads for Italy.

Where am I?

The music lures me toward the ornately carved double doors, and I enter the expansive space. A large assembly has gathered for mass, but on the far wall, a life-size statue of Mary, the Mother of Jesus, draws my attention. The figure of the Blessed Virgin appears to look out over the attendees who are seated on padded pews.

She's simply dressed in a long white garment with a blue shawl draped over her shoulders. A lacey white scarf covers her head, which is topped with a crown of flowers. Mary, Queen of the Universe, as I would come to know her, welcomes me with extended arms.

Is she trying to tell me something?

Chapter Six – The Bear

The statue's saintly eyes gaze at me with compassion, and suddenly, love and hope engulf me.

Does Mother Mary know my dilemma?

Some of my Catholic friends say they ask Mary to pray for them during tough times. Maybe she would pray for me, too.

The music stops abruptly and shadowy figures file up the aisle, but I keep staring at the Virgin Mother until a strong Greco-Roman face approaches.

"Nikki Loveleigh? What are you doing here? I didn't know you were Catholic." My body shrinks when I glance into the blue-gray eyes of six-foot tall Joey Paul.

Of all the times to run into him… of all the times for him to talk to me. I feel fat; I feel worthless.

"I'm not." My feeble voice squeaks.

I back up into the vestibule, turn to bolt, and trip over a brass base holding a bowl of holy water. The flying liquid splashes onto a group of nuns, and the white ceramic container thumps to the floor. Scrambling to maintain an upright position, I'm forced to jump over the fallen pedestal.

"Nikki, wait!" Joey Paul calls to me as I stumble out the door into the consuming darkness.

Which way is home?

When the church is out of sight, I retrieve my cell phone and dial Laura for directions.

While walking, I weigh my options. My parents favor abortion, and it would solve my problem quickly. But… if I follow that path, can I live with the guilt for the rest of my life? I think not.

I haven't forgiven myself for lying to a teacher once, for accepting a dare to shoplift, or for racing on a dangerous highway. The shame of abortion would be unbearable.

Laura thinks adoption is the answer, but I'd be pregnant for nine months. I'd have to drop out of my senior year, and everyone would talk about me. If I give up the baby, I would constantly wonder what it looks like, and if he or she is happy?

Does that awful boy have any idea of the anguish I'm going through? Would he even care?

When I ponder the third option, keeping the baby, a gentle feeling overwhelms me. I picture my older cousin's rosy-cheeked little boy—his tiny hand grasping my finger, his little feet kicking with joy.

I'm jolted out of that vision when a selfish voice in my head supports the other side. *"What about your college plans and the career you want? You can't go to school, work, and care for a baby!"*

Am I self-centered?

Is my father egotistical for wanting a normal daughter, one who doesn't cause whispering behind his back? Is he so selfish he condones killing an unborn baby? Am I?

Good battles evil in my brain, and the hard questions defy answers. None of the options appeal to me.

Maybe the river was the answer.

The lights from my house glow in the distance, and I resign myself to think no more tonight. Mentally and physically exhausted, I climb the stairs and collapse onto the pink duvet coverlet my mom so lovingly sewed.

Drifting to sleep, I consider my sweet mother. It's unthinkable that she would have aborted me. Then, I reflect on Mother Mary, a virgin mother, a symbol of the Catholic Church.

Probably, I'd understand what she wanted to tell me if my family and I were Catholic.

Mom attends the Baptist church regularly, dad stays home mostly, and Bogey and I usually make excuses not to go. Although, I'll never forget the song I learned in Sunday School. "Jesus loves me, this I know… for the bible tells me so…"

* * * *

When I wake up on Monday morning, one thing is clear: I *must* have more time to make the right decision about this pregnancy.

Oooga! Oooga!

My cell phone honks, and I nearly jump out of my skin.

When I first heard the songs that grandfather Anders wrote a few years ago, I laughed and thought it would be cute to have a ringtone from "Don't Blow Your Horn at Me."

Now, I'm not so sure.

Scrambling from under the bed covers, I answer before the person leaves a message.

"Hello!" My voice drips with annoyance.

"Nikki?" A familiar male voice sends fight or flight adrenalin through my veins.

OMG! Should I hang up or act defensive?

"What?" I interject as much irritation as in my greeting. "How did you get my cell number?"

"From Charlie… he goes to my church… you know, St. Teresa of Avila, the one you attended last night,"

"I wasn't attending, Joey Paul. I just *happened* to be there." Now my voice slants toward sarcasm.

"Oh… Well, I called to see if you hurt yourself when you fell over the holy water bowl."

"What does it matter if I hurt myself?"

Has he heard about my condition? Lord, kill me now.

"Nikki, I didn't mean to upset you. I shouldn't have called." Joey Paul sounds concerned.

"Thanks." Then for some reason, I disconnect the call with a punch of my finger.

Why do I do things like that? It's almost like I don't want people to be nice to me. Tugging the bedcovers over my head, I replay his brief words in my mind and wonder: who would know if people have found out about me?

Dear little Carly, that's who. My best friend who's proud that her mom supplies her with birth control pills. Impish little Carly, who occasionally says, "You should get some, too."

"Not me," I remember saying.

"The pill" had side effects, and anyway, I'd never need them… Ha!

Touching speed-dial on my phone, I wait to hear Carly's tone when I question her.

"Carly?"

"Nikki… I was thinking of texting you. You'll never guess who asked Charlie for your number."

"Oh, I know all right. Joey Paul called this morning, and I was rude and hung up on him."

"Why?" She sounds puzzled. *Maybe she hasn't heard.*

"You honestly don't know why I didn't want to talk to him?"

"No, I thought you'd love hearing from him… by the way, did you hurt yourself when you fell in church?"

"I've got to go, Carly. Good-bye." I tap the end-call button gently, this time.

She doesn't know I'm pregnant. The news hasn't spread, so if I go into hiding, possibly no one will ever find out.

I dial my new confidante, the voice of reason.

"Laurie?"

"Nikki. How are you this morning?"

"Fine. Have you contacted that family yet?"

"Come over, and we'll discuss it."

I gobble down cereal and make up a flimsy excuse to see Laura.

Plodding up her hilly driveway, I'm thankful that my morning sickness has subsided. At least, I feel good now, and a tentative plan has formed in my head. I'll live with the Cherokee family until it's too late for an abortion. Then, I'll visit my good-hearted grandma and grandpa Anders in Florida. Right now, adoption seems like the smartest choice for the baby and for me.

I don't really know the exact moment I decided against abortion. However, seeing the statue of Mary and thinking about her life has inspired me.

It could be that Laura's right; my baby has a destiny.

I sense a parallel between Mary and me.

Laura lays out the details for me to meet Joe and Hannah Braveheart. Tomorrow night at 7:00 pm, the couple will come to the casino, a public place crawling with people. I'm supposed to wear something red, and they'll wear fringed, white leather jackets.

Back home, I pack a few things and imagine myself in colorful Cherokee dresses when my own clothes don't fit. At first, the new adventure excites me. Then, I remember the reason and continue my preparations somberly.

Mulling over the runaway story that Laura and I concocted, I hope my parents won't be too shocked. After all, I have threatened to leave home and get a job until the baby comes. I've saved enough money to rent a room.

Tonight, I'll leave a note on my bed and ask them not to look for me. Mother will be devastated, but if I stay, my frail state of mind may not be able to stand up to dad's bullying.

I need time alone to confirm my decision. Mom says I have a few weeks to change my mind about an abortion. Is adoption really the way to go or is keeping the baby possible? Dad would probably kick me out of the house.

Stress builds in my head.

I decide to walk to St. Teresa of Avila church to see Mary's statue again, to calm my nerves and to help me think clearly. Striking out in the direction I took last night, I soon realize that things look different in daylight. Maple and elm trees line every sidewalk; pink flowering shrubs border red brick houses; American flags wave gingerly on their poles.

Reaching for my phone to google the name of the street, I find empty pockets.

Rats! I left my cell phone charging.

Suddenly, an old, dusty Lincoln loaded with teenage boys pulls up beside me.

"Hi, Nikki. Need a ride?"

Staring into a car of unfamiliar male faces, I'm puzzled. *Do I know any of them?*

"How do you know my name? Have we met?"

The older-looking boy in the front seat answers. "Sure, at Charlie's pool party. Don't you remember?"

"No, I don't!" I blast him with my snooty voice and continue walking while smoky fumes from their jalopy overtake me.

"Hop in. We'll give you a ride anywhere you want to go." His smooth words sound convincing.

I remember that Charlie introduced me to a cousin. Glancing back at the occupants of the slow-moving car, I notice the boy's eyes gleam in a weird way.

What did that cousin look like?

On the night of the party, I was too busy eyeing Joey Paul and Wolfie to notice anyone else.

"Are you from Asheville?"

He hesitates. "Uh… yeah, but I used to live here."

"Do you know how to get to St. Teresa of Avila church?"

"I do!" A voice speaks up from somewhere inside the car.

"Oh, sure… we know the street. Get in." The older one jumps out of the car and introduces himself as "Rabbit."

My instincts whisper not to trust this guy, but I don't heed the warning.

Ushering me into the back seat, he presents me to the other boys: "Owl," a sweet-looking kid, "Skunk," a roughly-dressed farm boy, and "Horse," a hefty weight-lifter type. All nicknames, I decide.

Have I made a mistake by getting into this car?

Horse drives to the main highway and speeds toward the mountains.

Horrified, I scream. "What are you doing? The church is in town, not out here!"

"Just taking a little ride." Rabbit jokes.

"Take her back!" Owl shouts.

Owl has big, honest black eyes and straight black hair. No doubt, he's from Cherokee land. The others, I'm not sure.

"Not yet." Rabbit defies the command. "Drive, Horse."

"Stop!" I cry. "Let me out!" I rattle the door handle but the driver has control of the locks.

"Let her out, man!" Skunk yells.

"Pull over here, Horse." Rabbit directs the driver.

The car stops halfway up the mountain, and the dark forest bounds on both sides. Rabbit drags me out of the vehicle while Owl and Skunk shout for him to release me.

I kick, scream, and fight as he wrestles me along an old fire trail laden with pine needles. The farther we go into the woods, I know my fate is sealed.

Mother Mary, pray for me.

Will he kill me afterwards? I hope so.

He throws me to the ground, and instantly, a strong scent of cinnamon overpowers my senses. I dare to open my eyes.

A giant black bear towers over Rabbit and me. The animal's huge mouth forms an oval, and with a dreadful roar, a spray of saliva and foul breath saturates the air.

My abductor jumps up and attempts to run, but he's no match for the bear. Caught like a kitten by the back of his neck, Rabbit screams. The wild beast shreds the boy's clothes with razor-sharp claws and pommels his floppy body with huge black paws.

"Stop!" I shriek.

The hairy creature drops his prey in a blood-stained heap and walks away. Leaving a fragrant trail of cinnamon, the bear disappears into the woods as quick as he appeared.

I scramble to my feet and brush dirt and leaves from my clothes, which are still intact. *Thank you, Jesus.*

Somewhere above, a twig snaps. I glance up and see Kimi Wesa perched on the limb of a large oak tree. Her jewel-green eyes fix on me, and for the first time, I notice a distinct M shape on the cat's forehead. *What could it mean?*

A commotion on the ground distracts me, and I see Skunk, Owl, and Horse helping their bloody companion to his feet.

Owl gazes at me with tears in his eyes. "Are you okay?"

"I'm fine. Just go! I can find my way home."

"I'll stay with you," he offers.

"No!" I wave my arms for them to leave, and they drag Rabbit back to the car.

Shaken and disgusted with myself for trusting them, I wait for the screech of speeding tires. Satisfied that evil has left the forest, I look back at the tree limb, but Kimi has vanished.

No more woods for me today. I trek along the edge of the highway, back to the city limits. Every now and then, I catch the image of a soaring eagle like it's accompanying me home, and I wonder…

Did Adawehi shapeshift into a bear to save me, or did he direct the bear, or was it all a coincidence?

For the rest of the day, a fog envelops my brain. I muddle through chores, change bed sheets, wash clothes, and dust my room like a robot. By dinner time, my senses return. Should I report the kidnapping to someone?

My dad? He'd either want to kill the boys or not believe

me. The police? That whole scene would be trouble for the blameless boys. Besides, I think Rabbit learned his lesson. He won't be trying to rape anyone else.

And, *I* learned to listen to my inner voice.

* * * *

The next morning, news reports of a rogue bear attack rumble through the house. At breakfast, mom cautions me not to go into the woods. Apparently, three local hikers have been treated for shock and released from the hospital. A fourth person has sustained serious scratches but no life-threatening injuries.

Smiling at the thought of the bear, I'm certain Adawehi wouldn't have gravely wounded my assailant.

And the cat...? Why does Kimi Wesa have the letter M on her forehead?

* * * *

Nightfall finds me clutching my floral carryall purse in the bustling casino lobby. I wheel my leopard-print luggage behind me and search every which way for white-leather jackets.

Noise from the slot machines in the gaming area deafens me, stench from stale cigarette smoke nauseates me, and the glaring orange, yellow, and green carpet flashes in my eyes like a strobe light.

No matter, my underage ID prohibits entry into the gambling section, and the Bravehearts wouldn't look for me there, anyway.

Dodging tourists, hotel guests, and casino personnel, I

mill around the lounge area, gift shops, and eateries hoping to spot the Bravehearts. The meeting place should've been more specific; this place is ginormous!

Earlier that evening, after leaving the note on my neatly made bed, I had hopped into Laura's Crosstrek parked near Charlie's house. During the short ride, she drove silently, and I reflected on being a runaway, which left no time to discuss the events of the past twenty-four hours.

With hugs and words of encouragement, she dropped me in front of the Cherokee casino and left in a hurry. We didn't know anyone who gambled, but just in case, we didn't want people to suspect Laura had helped me escape.

Soon, Joe and Hannah Braveheart glide into the main lobby with white-leather fringe swinging, and my jittery nerves flip-flop like Mexican jumping beans. Do I really want to do this?

But wait... who's that with them?

Chapter Seven – Oliver

Owl? This is not good.

I scoot behind a bushy fichus tree before my red sweater labels me. Jerking the tell-tale garment from my arms, I stuff it into the cloth carryall.

What is Owl doing with the Bravehearts? I can't go through with this now, no way.

I slip into a sundries shop, roll my suitcase out of view, and make an attempt to blend in with the magazines and books.

Regrettably, Owl's sharp black eyes don't miss a thing. "Nikki?"

"Oh… it's you." Glancing up briefly, I back up a little, bury my face in a periodical, and avoid direct eye contact.

"What are you doing at the casino?" He sounds truly surprised.

"What are *you* doing at the casino?" I fire back.

"I'm with my foster parents, the Bravehearts. They're here to help someone… an unfortunate girl." He turns away shyly.

Searching my brain for something to say, all I come up with is "Oh," again.

"Have you seen a girl wearing red?" Owl asks.

"Uh… no… Owl… but that's not your real name, is it?" I change the subject.

"It's Oliver. Oliver Rainchild. Joe and Hannah found me on their doorstep in the pouring rain and gave me that last name." He pauses. "That guy, Rabbit… uh… his real name is Randolph. He made up those nicknames. He said I had big owl eyes.

"I didn't mind too much. The Cherokee believe owls have reached a state of purity in the animal kingdom." Oliver looks around and lowers his voice to a whisper.

"I'm so sorry about Randolph… taking you… and… everything that happened yesterday." He touches my shoulder tenderly, and I see sincerity in his sweet face.

"Randolph and Horse offered to give me a ride home. I didn't know they could do something like… kidnapping." Oliver frowns and shakes his head in disgust.

"It was partly my fault for getting in the car." I shrug.

"You did nothing wrong." Oliver's voice grows louder. "Did you report him to the police?"

"I thought about it, but my father would probably kill Randolph if he knew."

"You weren't hurt, were you… by Rabbit or the bear?" Oliver gazes at me.

"No…"

"Oliver?" A woman's voice interrupts our conversation.

Joe and Hannah Braveheart breeze into the shop. "Have you seen the young lady in red?" Joe questions his foster son.

"Hello." Mrs. Braveheart speaks when she realizes I'm standing with Oliver.

"Hi." I look down at my shoes and silently thank heaven that I didn't wear the red ones.

"No." Oliver answers Joe and then introduces me. "Uh... Joe, Hannah, this is Nikki." They both nod, smile, and shake my hand.

"We'll walk around the garden and pool area. If you see the girl in red, tell her to wait in the lobby." Hannah looks me up and down before they leave.

My eyes dart to the suitcase propped behind the book rack.

Did her shrewd eyes spot it there?

Oliver and I chat for a few more minutes, and I'm amazed at his good heart. On Saturdays, he weeds the community vegetable garden for the homeless, and after school on Wednesdays, he reads to dogs at the no-kill-shelter. For sure, Oliver Rainchild wouldn't participate in a kidnapping or a rape.

"Why did you say you were here?" He repeats his earlier question.

"I didn't. Actually... I was waiting for my... cousin. But she's very late, so I think I'll just go home." With an excuse now, I roll my animal-print luggage into view.

"Do you need a ride?" He doesn't question my unlikely reason for being in the casino.

"No, I'll call my friend Laura."

"I'm sure Joe and Hannah won't mind taking you home."

I accept his offer, and we stroll outside to find the Bravehearts as we continue to get acquainted.

Oliver is eighteen and attends the Qualla Boundary high school, even though his sweet, dimpled face appears younger. Also, I learn that Oliver Rainchild's teachers have recommended him for a full scholarship to Juilliard, a famous music college in New York City.

Wow! He must be really smart.

In the midst of our conversation, I sense we're being watched. I glance to my right and see Kimi Wesa beneath a topiary bush a few feet away.

"Do you see that big cat?"

"Yes, of course." Oliver nods.

"Do you see the M on her forehead?" I point.

"There's a legend behind that M..." Oliver hesitates, but I motion for him to continue. "As the story goes, after Mother Mary wrapped baby Jesus with blankets and laid him in a manager, he cried.

"A cat heard the baby crying, hopped into the crib, snuggled up to the infant, and kept Jesus warm.

"Grateful for the cat's kindness, Mary stroked the animal and put her mark on its forehead. Even today, she reminds us of her gratitude with a M on every cat."

"That's a delightful story. I'll have to check out every cat I see." I turn toward the topiary, but Kimi is gone.

"Oliver? It's been almost an hour and we haven't found the girl. We can't wait much longer." Hannah Braveheart studies my luggage when she finds us on a garden bench near the large statue of a Cherokee Indian head.

She flashes a questioning look, and I stutter my response.

"I... I... was supposed to stay a week with my... cousin, but she never showed up." My eyelids quiver, and I look down at my sandals, again.

"Can we give her a ride to her house, Hannah?" Oliver ends the awkwardness with his question, and Hannah agrees.

Planning what to say in case mom found my note, I'm

quiet the whole way home. Just a mumbled "Yes" and "Thank you" gets me through it.

To avoid any conflict with my father, I ask the Bravehearts to drop me off at Charlie's driveway since it's only a couple hundred feet from mine. Hovering by his mailbox like it marks the entrance to *my* house, I wave good-bye to the charitable couple and their foster son.

On this warm June evening, distant sirens prompt me to sprint through the dark night and dash up our new asphalt driveway.

At my front door, I retrieve a spare key from the specified geranium pot, slip it into the lock, and tiptoe to my room. Puzzled to discover my note missing, I glance at the time. Mom usually says goodnight much later than 9 o'clock.

Footsteps scuffle lightly down the hallway, and I dart my eyes to the door. As I watch and listen, a lined sheet of notebook paper slides underneath.

Bogey!

He demands ransom.

If you want your note back, pay me $20!
Guess who

That little blackmailer! I jerk the door open, but he's nowhere in sight. Crumpling the paper into a wad, I pitch it into the wastebasket. On second thought, I grab it and rip it to pieces. He won't show my note to mom and dad yet. He'll wait for the money.

Sitting on the bed, I rub aloe lotion on my tired legs, but I'm exhausted. My eyes droop, and I fall flat on my pillow until my cell phone jolts me out of deep slumber.

Oooga!

"Where are you?" Laura speaks in a panic before I can say hello.

I open my sandpapered eyes and respond with slurred words. "I'm home. A boy named Oliver was with the Bravehearts, and I couldn't go through with it."

Laura's words spill fast and furious. "Hannah Braveheart called me and said the girl didn't show up. I was afraid something had happened to you. What are you going to do now?"

"We'll figure out something else. Let's talk in the morning." I say goodnight and hang up.

Laura arrives at our house bright and early, and mom offers homemade pecan waffles with blueberries.

My friend leans toward me and whispers. "Why are these so-o-o good?"

"Real butter and pure maple syrup," I say, cramming my mouth full.

My father finishes his waffles in a hurry and leaves for the barn.

"Remember you're still grounded, Miss Nikki!" he mocks.

"Dad…" I try to protest, but he slams the door.

Talking and soaking up rays, the voice of reason and I lounge by the pool. With Bogey at a friend's house, we enjoy the peace and quiet. On such a beautiful, sunny day, it's not hard to imagine that we're living in a perfect world… except we're not.

Laura and I discuss my dilemma, and I divulge the whole kidnapping thing, the bear attack, and how I met Oliver.

My confidante listens without taking her eyes off me. Her mind clicks, calculates, and files away every detail. Hopefully, Laura will continue to help me deal with all that's happening.

Then, Laura shocks me. "You know… Hannah suspects their foster son's friend is the girl they were supposed to meet."

"What? How could she? I wasn't wearing anything red when she saw me."

"Hannah noticed something red stuffed in your cloth purse, and she said the girl seemed nervous."

"You didn't tell her my name, did you?" Frowning at Laura, I sit up straight.

"No, of course not. We never discuss identities over the phone. Hannah has strict privacy rules about the people she and Joe help."

"What should I do? And how well do you know them anyway?"

"My mom's a social worker, and sometimes, she refers children to the Bravehearts. You should confide in Hannah. She'll keep whatever you say confidential." Laura's logic makes sense, and I consider her idea.

"I don't want Oliver to know… about my condition… he's really nice. Why did this happen to me?" I sob.

Oooga! Oooga!

My cell phone interrupts our conversation, but I don't recognize the number.

"Hello?" I answer, cautiously questioning.

"Nikki, it's me, Oliver." A gentle male voice reassures me.

I remember he asked for my phone number, to keep in touch, and a wave of calm engulfs me.

"Oh… Hi, Oliver." I respond with the fresh, sweetness of puppy love.

Laura rolls her eyes and muffles a giggle.

"Wanna do something today… or tomorrow?" His voice

rings of innocence. "We could go swimming, or hiking, or something."

"I'm sort of grounded for the summer... for going to Charlie Quinn's last-day-of-school pool party and... well... other stuff. I don't remember seeing you at the party."

Laura leans in to listen.

"No, I don't know Charlie," he says.

"That's good!" I grimace after realizing my relief sounds odd.

Yay! The black shoe isn't his.

"Besides, I was probably practicing for the July 4th concert." Thankfully, Oliver didn't seem to pick up on my comment.

"Oh, yeah... sorry I missed it. What instrument did you play?" I encourage him to keep talking, unlike the time I rudely ended a call from Joey Paul.

"I played the cello then."

"What others do you play?"

"Mostly string instruments... guitar, violin, bass, and steel guitar. Would you like to sit with my family at the Labor Day concert in September?"

"Yes, I would." I don't hesitate to think about my answer.

Laura frowns.

Rats! Will I be fat by September? Maybe I should *get an abortion.*

Selfish thoughts enter my head, and I can't deal with them right now.

"I have to... go, Oliver. I have to... hang up." My eyelids quiver, and my words become choppy and brusque.

"No, wait. Hannah wants to invite you to dinner tomorrow night."

"Really?" Questions and scenarios fill my mind. Will

Hannah try to "talk" to me? Will she ask me to help in the kitchen and then accuse me of being the girl that was supposed to wear red?

"Your dad will let you go to dinner, right? I'll still be at music practice, but Hannah can pick you up at 5:30." His voice is sweet, and I don't want to say no.

All-knowing Laura hears the invitation, smiles, and nods yes.

"I think so. Tell her to meet me at the same place she dropped me off last night." I accept the offer with no intention of asking dad's permission.

After we say good-bye, I settle back in my chair and gaze at Laura. "Laurie, why did I agree to have dinner with his family? What have I done?"

"It's an opportunity to talk to Hannah. And… you know, Oliver has to be informed of your situation, the sooner the better." Laura's green eyes glint in the sun, and she raises an approving eyebrow.

What other choice do I have? Certainly, running away to an unknown place would take more courage than I can muster.

While I ponder Laura's point, my mother enters the pool area and says she made an appointment to discuss a possible abortion.

"When?" I scream.

Suddenly, the chlorine odor from the pool nauseates me.

"On Tuesday, at 2:00," she says. "We're only going to talk about your options."

"That's only a few days away!" Leaving Laura to fend for herself, I leap from my chaise lounge, sprint up the stairs, slam my door, and vomit.

* * * *

The next day, I stay in my room with the door locked. I've forgotten about my brother and his ransom note.

Rattle, rattle... Knock, knock.

I open for Bogey who's holding my note in one hand and a shabby catcher's mitt in the other.

With soft brown, tousled hair and a sweaty-from-play-ing-outside smell, he pleads his case.

"I'm short 20 bucks for a new mitt." His sheepish grin confirms what I knew all along; he wouldn't rat me out.

"Okay." I reach for my purse.

Our grandparents give generous gifts of cash on birthdays and Christmas. I save my money, but Bogey buys video games, ice cream, and graphic comic books.

Extending one hand to retrieve my note and the other hand to offer the $20, I smile at my little brother. He's not so bad... for a brother.

"I'm glad you didn't go," he muttered.

* * * *

Sneaking out of the house at meal time isn't easy. So, I say I need to see Laura.

"Don't hold dinner... I'm nauseas anyway." That part is no lie. The odor of greasy pork chops has never agreed with me.

Not wanting Hannah to wait, I leave at 5:15. If she rings Charlie's doorbell, it wouldn't be good. Wondering what we'll talk about in the car, I regret not thinking this through.

Sure enough, she's early. When I round the curve of the

road, her silver Santa Fe idles near the Quinn's mailbox. I walk faster.

"Hi!" Hannah greets me as I approach the car. "Am I too early?"

"No, no, I was just... uh... taking a walk."

To my relief, the ride to the Braveheart's house is short, no time to bring up "my condition."

My mouth drops open at the sight of their two-story white-frame home, freshly mowed grass, trimmed box-woods, and tidy beds of yellow, purple, and blue iris... not what I expected. I guess all of Qualla Boundary isn't poverty-stricken.

Hannah sees my expression and explains that Joe serves as one of the chiefs. The larger house allows them to foster needy children whenever the occasion arises.

Within minutes, Oliver and Joe arrive home. A modest meal of corn cakes, green beans, and barbequed chicken wings nourishes the four of us at the Braveheart's claw-footed oak table. We laugh, and the conversation flows until Joe asks me about my college plans.

Fidgeting awkwardly, I gaze out their picture window and spot a large gray-striped cat with a poufy fur mane. *Kimi Wesa?*

"It's a bit early to think of college, right, Nikki?" Hannah comes to my rescue and changes the discussion to Oliver's plans.

She knows I'm the pregnant girl.

"Oliver hopes to attend the Juilliard School of Music on a scholarship, but he still has another year at the Qualla Boundary high school." Hannah studies my face like she's trying to read my thoughts.

"Do you have a cat?" I lay my fork down and question my new friend's foster mom.

"No, why?" asks Hannah.

"A big cat is watching us through the window."

Oliver and his family turn toward the glass, but Kimi has vanished.

Chapter Eight – The Blessed Virgin

"Was it the cat we saw at the casino?" Oliver studies me with striking black eyes.

"I'm pretty sure… but how did it get here, miles away?"

"That same gray cat hangs around the house sometimes. I took it some meat scraps one day, but it had disappeared." My friend continues to gaze at me like a boy with a new puppy.

"Probably just a stray…. Would you like to help clear the table, Nikki?" Hannah jumps up and busies herself with the dishes.

I nod and pick up the plates. Walking into the kitchen, I notice a small desk with a statue of Mother Mary, the Blessed Virgin, and several rosaries hanging on the wall. Stopping to study the articles, I question Hannah.

"Are you Catholic?"

"Yes, we go to St. Teresa of Avila in town. I haven't seen you…"

"My family is Baptist, but recently, the music drew me into your church, and I was mesmerized by Mary's statue. I felt like she wanted to tell me something, but then I tripped over a bowl of holy water and exited pretty quickly." We both laughed. Hannah's gentle nature puts me at ease.

"So, that was you? I heard about the incident, but no harm was done." Hannah looks at me with serious, loving eyes. "Do you want to talk about why you admired the Blessed Virgin?"

I glance toward the living room and see Oliver and Joe watching the sports news on TV.

"I would… like to tell you everything but not here," I whisper.

"Let's get a cup of cocoa and go upstairs. I'll show you my needlepoint and the shawls I'm knitting for the Elder Home." Hannah raises her voice, probably in case the guys wonder where we went.

In her sewing room, two small wing chairs face each other with a small round table in the middle, just right for chatting and sipping after-dinner cocoa. When she closes the door, I sob uncontrollably.

Hannah consoles me, and I tell my story, ending with changing my mind at the casino. The only thing I leave out is Rabbit and the bear encounter.

This kind Cherokee lady sits in silence for a minute.

"I believe I can convince your father to let you live here until the birth. Then the Catholic Adoption Charity can take over, if that's what you decide. First though, I want to show you another statue of Mary."

"You'd let me live here even if I'm not Cherokee?" Bleakly, I look up from watery eyes.

"Of course, Laura's mother has done many favors for us."

"But what about Oliver? Won't it be awkward for him… and me?" I search her eyes for a compromising answer.

"Don't worry, God's plan has a way of working things out." Hannah dismisses my question for the moment. "Now, let's get going. The dishes can wait."

After I say good-bye to Joe and Oliver, Hannah Braveheart drives us to St. Teresa of Avila. As daylight fades, she pulls around to a shed in back of the church.

"I think this is what Mother Mary wanted you to know." She points to a family of life-size statues gathered around a nativity scene.

As I gaze at the traditional Christmas figures, the dust from last season's scattered straw teases my nose, and I sneeze. Through itchy eyes, I see a proud Mary, a gentle Joseph, the three kings, a shepherd, and baby Jesus, all painted in primary blues, reds, and yellows. Standing erect, they silently wait for the next joyful birth celebration.

Speechless, I stare at the colorful group.

The Blessed Mother was a virgin just like I was a virgin. It turned out okay for her... she had Jesus!

"We store the statues here for our Christmas exhibition. We also bring in live barnyard animals. Have you ever visited our nativity scene in front of the church?"

"No." My eyes won't budge from the baby... and his family.

It makes sense now. Adawehi and Mother Mary want me to keep my baby, and a soft, inner voice whispers that the baby could grow up to accomplish great things.

The darker voice in my head says, "Listen to your father. You're too young to care for a baby. Get rid of it, one way or another!"

I cry. I weep. I moan.

Hannah helps me to her car, and to my surprise, she drives to a homemade ice cream parlor.

"Something cool will soothe our souls." She regards me with an empathetic expression.

We sit outside on a picnic bench and savor our favorites; a cup of coconut almond for me and rocky road for Hannah. After the cold treat, I feel much calmer.

Hannah Braveheart and I remain a while longer and talk about lots of things, not just babies and pregnancies. She tells me about her past, which made her a loving, caring woman who helps children.

Hannah's first husband mistreated her and their daughter who grew up and moved away. Hannah feared the man and didn't have the courage to stand up to his verbal and emotional abuse.

However, her second marriage is a match made in heaven, and they've vowed to bring love, peace, and joy to as many families and children as possible. According to Hannah, she and Joe didn't hesitate to take in Oliver when he was left on their doorstep eighteen years ago.

It sounds like the couple have loved him like a biological son and have nurtured all of their foster children, as well.

I tell Hannah about my life, which hasn't always been explosive, and my school friends.

When my brother and I were younger, our family went on picnics. We vacationed at grandpa Loveleigh's lake house, and dad trailered our horses for Bogey and me to ride in horse shows.

Hannah laughs at how my quirky friend, Carly, gets us into trouble, and how the younger Gary and Sammy like to hang out with us.

I express my fondness for the Cherokee children I met at vacation bible school, and Hannah's rich brown eyes light up with a deepened interest in me.

"Oh dear, look at the time. We need to do this tonight. You can pack a few things and come back with me to Qualla Boundary." Hastily, she tosses the empty ice cream cups into a trash can.

"But, my father…" I picture the disgust on his face when Hannah suggests I come and live with her and Joe on Cherokee land. He's never been accepting of people different from us.

"Let me handle it." Her confident tone reassures me.

* * * *

It's 9pm. We go into the house through the kitchen door, and dad has just finished dinner.

"What the…?" He looks confused and miffed when I walk in with the American Indian lady.

But… always a charmer to strangers, he invites her into the living room and sits quietly until she states her reason for being there. At that moment, my father's eyes twitch, his upper lip curls, and a scornful frown covers his face.

Hannah's words drive directly to the point and her professional manner is impeccable. She ends her case by stating that she's certain he wants the very best for his only daughter.

"Hell, no!" dad yells. "No, she can't live with you! She has an appointment for an abortion next week!"

"Vern," my mother interrupts. "The appointment is a consultation to discuss our options."

"What *options*? She's getting rid of it and soon!" He snorts around the room like a mad bull, huffing and puffing.

Hannah remains calm, and I draw my strength from her.

"Dad, I don't want to kill the baby. I may want to give it

up for adoption; I'm not sure yet. Whatever I decide will be my decision and no one else's.

"Living with Hannah and Joe Braveheart is best for me at this point in time. It will give me the peace to think." I solemnly state my intention in a quiet manner.

A hush falls over the room, interrupted only by the loud tick of my great grandmother's mantle clock.

My mother hugs me and silent tears stream down her cheeks. She nods her approval of the plan and whispers softly. "I support you in anything you choose, and I'll visit you every week."

For a few minutes, Dad stares out the living room window into a black night sky. Then…

"How will she finish high school?" He sounds more civilized now.

"I'm certified in the state of North Carolina for home schooling and have taught many children in the past." Hannah glances at me and winks.

With his back turned, he waves his hand to dismiss us. My father has given up; he's outnumbered and done with arguing.

"But… she can't take the corvette! It's registered in my name." My father throws one final blow, like having the last laugh.

Who cares! I'm free!

Gleefully, I sprint up the stairs to gather my clothes, and mom and Hannah follow close behind.

Bogey sits on the top step, listening.

Seeing his sad, young face, I realize this is a turning point in my life, and my joy subsides. I'm leaving my home, perhaps never to return.

* * * *

After the soundest sleep I've had in weeks, I awake in the Braveheart house to the aroma of pancakes. Dressing quickly, I skip down the steps to the bright yellow kitchen.

My new family sits at their large, round oak table and greets me with happy faces. I feel more relaxed already, and apparently, Hannah has briefed Oliver on why I'm here.

Our eyes meet and he smiles approvingly. I'm embarrassed but relieved that he knows my condition.

Later that morning, on the front porch, Oliver sits and watches while I do needlework. On a piece of needlepoint canvas, I've painted a large gray cat sitting on a tree branch. Now, I'm matching yarn to the various colors and pulling it through the tiny holes.

"That's the Norwegian Forest cat we saw at the casino and in the yard, right?" Oliver studies the painting.

"Yes, her name is Kimi Wesa."

"That's Cherokee for secret cat. Do you know the language?" Oliver's face is uncomfortably close to mine.

I hope he doesn't notice the pimple I saw in the mirror this morning.

"Not really... uh... someone told me her name. But... I'd rather talk about that some other time." I concentrate on my needlework.

"What else do you like to do?" He looks down at my bagful of paints and papers.

"Oh... reading, knitting, and writing." Thinking he couldn't really be interested in my hobbies, I avoid eye contact.

"What kind of writing?" Oliver scoots his chair even closer.

"I've written poems and song lyrics, but the music part is just in my head."

"Maybe we can help each other. Sometimes, I have trouble fitting words to my music." Oliver's voice pitches higher, and his excitement gains my attention.

We lock eyes.

The moment ends when a mail truck rounds the corner and stops at the Braveheart's mailbox. Oliver meets the mailman and stares at a large manila envelope.

He rushes to the front door. "Hannah! Come, look at this!"

She comes quickly, and they rip open the packet.

"You're in! Juilliard has granted you a full scholarship and accepted you for early admission." Hannah hugs Oliver, and they jump around like little kids.

"So, you won't be attending Qualla Boundary High School this fall?" I peek over his shoulder at the college logo.

"No, I'll skip my senior year and start classes at Juilliard in August." Grinning, he stares at the words on the letter.

Remembering what Hannah said about God's plan, I glance at her.

She smiles.

This means Oliver, the boy I've begun to like more and more, won't be here to watch me waddle around with a huge stomach.

Thank you, Jesus!

Chapter Nine –
The Kidnapping

August arrives and preparations begin for Oliver's journey to Juilliard. Excited for their foster son's opportunity, the Bravehearts eagerly map a driving route to New York City.

Oliver is assigned to a residence hall, and none of the family want to sightsee in the "Big Apple." So, Joe and Hannah plan a quick trip.

A long, hot ride to New York and back is not appealing to me. I still hurl my meals from time to time, and soon, my first trimester tummy will be bulging. Besides, no one suggests I come along.

Most of my jeans still fit, but occasionally, mom brings new items of loose clothing. She calls and visits often, and sometimes, Bogey comes with her. I think he misses me. Nevertheless, my dad has neither called nor dropped by.

A few weeks have passed since I moved into the Bravehearts's home. Joe and Hannah treat me like I'm carrying a miracle, not like I have a shameful condition. I've found peace, love, and joy, and my decision not to abort the baby stands firm. Everyone here agrees, even Oliver.

Oliver and I discuss everything openly when we work on music for my lyrics and words for his compositions.

"Let's include the sounds you heard in the forest... just before the angel appeared and said you were fertile." Oliver often encourages me during our sessions.

I recall being reluctant to talk about it at first, but now Oliver knows every detail and accepts the truth as I see it. He even believes Adawehi shape-shifted into a bear to save me from being raped by Rabbit. Oliver listens intently and advises gently, earning the title of my *new* voice of reason and best friend.

"When awkward moments happen, hold your head high and look people in the eye. You were the victim. None of this was your fault." His counseling gives me self-confidence.

I had told him about dodging Joey Paul at church and slipping out into the dark night.

Once, Wolfie had called while I was plunking on the keyboard, and Oliver was writing down the notes. The tall, dark, and handsome Cherokee/Italian wanted to talk. "No, I'm sorry. I can't," I blurted, then quickly hung up.

My new confidante says it's okay to talk with friends. However, Wolfie hasn't called again, and I haven't run into Joey Paul lately.

Somehow, my romantic interest in Wolfie and Joey Paul has waned. I guess I've outgrown those crushes.

* * * *

The morning arrives for Oliver, Joe, and Hannah to drive to New York. They jot down a list of emergency phone numbers, write the trash pick-up schedule on the kitchen blackboard, and hug me goodbye. Oliver's embrace sends thrills through my spine. He gazes into my eyes, pecks me on the cheek, and says, "Everything will be okay."

What does he mean... everything?

As I watch the loaded car pull away with my extended family, an uneasy feeling envelops me. After locking the doors, I concentrate on my household chores and hobbies for the rest of the day. I straighten my room, tackle my needlepoint, paint a picture of the old Cherokee man, and write words to a new song.

That night, I wake up sweating from a nightmare. In the dream, a large spaceship lands in the yard, and an alien creature climbs out and lumbers toward me. With huge spiraling eyes, it stares into my face and hoarsely moans, "Beware of the dark."

Frightened by the realistic image, I bolt upright and glance out my window at the moonlit landscape below. Kimi Wesa perches high in the large oak tree that shades the Braveheart's yard on sunny days.

Has my imagination kicked in because of the dream, or do the cat's glowing eyes flash a warning? Blink blink... blink blink blink... blink blink.

Wide awake now, I tiptoe down to the shadowy kitchen in my bare feet, open the refrigerator, and pour a glass of milk. A gloved hand covers my mouth, and I drop the glass.

I struggle to scream, but the hand tightens over my face and pinches my nose with a piece of cloth. The stifling stench of ether enters my nostrils, and I pass out.

* * * *

Early morning light enters through the narrow slits of my

eyes, and slowly, I study the bare concrete-block walls of an unfinished basement.

Where am I? Who did this?

Being more angry than afraid, I twist and turn the rope that ties my wrists and project muffled sounds through the duct-tape that covers my mouth. "Hehwahwah... hehwahwah!"

It's no use. The rope isn't budging, and no one will be able to understand my pitiful noises.

Attempting to rise from the yellow air mattress between me and the cold floor, I pull my knees up to my chest and roll onto my side. With my face smashed into the inflated rubber mat, I wriggle and heave myself erect.

Creak... k... k. A door opens at the top of the stairs. Someone *has* heard my weak protest.

"Well, well, look who woke up? If it isn't the girl with the trained bear." A chillingly familiar male voice mocks me. "How did you control that beast? Are you a witch or a voodoo priestess?"

Now, I'm frightened. His slow, creepy footfall on each squeaky wooden tread triggers an alarm in my head.

Mother Mary, pray for me.

But wait... he trips over something.

Plunk! Plunk! Kerplunk!

Randolph, aka Rabbit, tumbles down the basement steps while a sleek, shadowy animal nips at his sprawling body. I can't identify the creature for lack of light. Yet, I hear it plainly, and its distinct musty wild odor claims this underground space.

"Gr-r-r-r." A deep, throaty, growl sends shivers through my backbone.

Whatever is snarling, doesn't care for Rabbit. Together,

they splat on the floor, and the animal tears into my abductor's leg like a cartoon Tasmanian devil with spit and hair flying.

I focus on the growling shape and recognize it as a cougar, which is native to the Great Smoky Mountains.

How did a wild cougar get into this house?

Randolph screams and jumps up, kicking. The terrified man clambers halfway up the stairs, but the animal attacks his legs from the rear. Tangled with the cougar, Randolph falls backward and bangs his head hard on the concrete floor.

The wild cat scrambles to its feet, sprints up the steps, and springs through the open basement door.

With my hands bound behind me, I sidestep Randolph's bashed body as quickly as I can and struggle up the stairs, two steps at a time. It feels totally awkward and unbalanced, but it works.

Lightheaded from skipping steps, I watch as the cougar slams against a screen door, dashes from the house, and races into the woods.

Woozily, I stare at the battered door and recognize the Braveheart's kitchen. If only I had heeded Kimi's warning or believed my nightmare, maybe I could have avoided being drugged and tied up in the basement.

Realizing I should call the police, I stumble to the wall phone and knock the receiver off with my jaw. Even though it hurts, I push 911 with the bridge of my nose.

"What is your emergency?" The dispatcher answers my call.

"Hel-l-l E-e-e! L-l-e-e-s-s-s!" My taped mouth can't form p's or m's.

"I can't understand you. Are you in trouble?"

"E-s-s-s! U-r-r-r-y!" I plead with all the urgency I can muster.

"I see you're calling from the Braveheart's house. Is that correct?"

"E-s-s-s!" L-l-e-e-s-s-s, u-r-r-ry!"

"Help should arrive in three minutes. Go to a safe place and wait."

Bumping what's left of the screen door with my shoulder, I stagger to the front yard and plop onto the grass next to the street. When I'm seated, I notice that same dusty old Lincoln parked in the driveway.

A confused face peers out from the driver's side window, and the car door swings open. The boy nicknamed Horse runs toward me.

"Are you okay? I'm so-o-o sorry. Rabbit swore he only wanted to scare you." Horse's sympathetic eyes tell me he's the kind of guy who would place an air mattress between an unconscious girl and a cold concrete floor.

Horse carefully removes the tape from my mouth and unties my wrists. Within seconds, the blaring sirens and flashing blue lights of police cars round the curve and bring pajama-clad neighbors out onto their porches.

At the same time, a bleeding Randolph hobbles out of the house and yells for Horse to drive him to a hospital. When Horse refuses, the injured man limps hurriedly toward the forest, only to be tackled by two police officers.

After I give my statement, the policemen arrest Randolph and take Horse, too, for being an accomplice to kidnapping. In the process, I hear Horse's real name.

"Thanks, Howard, for untying me."

He nods solemnly before he's handcuffed.

The police lieutenant advises me to get checked by a

doctor, but with no cuts or bruises, I refuse, thinking I am unharmed.

However, after the men leave, my hands quiver and a torrent of tears flow. Barely able to talk without sniffling and snuffling, I dial Laura.

It's still early, but she arrives within minutes and wants all the details. Only then, do I fully understand what could have happened to me and… my baby. No longer is it "nobody's baby." It's *my* baby, and I will protect her or him to the best of my ability.

When the house phone rings, I know it's Hannah. According to Laura, officers have to report a home invasion to the homeowners.

"Hello-o-o-o." I answer cheerfully to ease her mind.

Hannah wants to rent a car to come home and let the guys continue on to New York. Of course, I insist that I'm okay, so Hannah asks Laura to stay with me until they return, if it's alright with her mother.

Oliver sounds emotional, but I'm cheerful and upbeat and assure him of my well-being.

"I promise… I-I'll call you every day…" His throat chokes up.

Okay… where is this going? How can it possibly go any-where with me pregnant?

When the call ends, I glance out the living room window. Secret Cat sits on a low limb of the big oak tree, and her eyes twinkle with contentment. Truly, she's an angel watching over me.

"Look, Laurie. It's Kimi Wesa."

"Where?" Laura turns, but Kimi's image vanishes.

"I guess her name is Secret Cat because not everyone can see her." Disappointed, I frown and shrug.

That evening, Laura and I wolf down the fish stew and hot, buttered cornbread that her mom brought over. She eats with us and stays awhile to make sure we're comfortable to stay alone.

After Mrs. Acres leaves, Laura makes hot cocoa, and we discuss the probability that Kimi or Adawehi directed the cougar, just like they probably arranged the bear episode.

"Maybe the animals appeared by chance… but my some of my friends say there's no such thing as coincidences, only 'God incidents.'" Hoping to see Kimi again, I set down my cup and stare into the yard.

"Laurie, will you drive me to St. Teresa of Avila Church on Sunday? I want to thank Jesus for sending his angels to protect me, and I'd like to thank Mother Mary for her intercessions."

Chapter Ten – Court

Hannah and Joe decide to stay in New York for Juilliard's welcome dinner for parents. So, for the next few days, Laura and I laugh, play games, pull weeds, plant flowers, paint pictures, and attend mass at church.

Mom visits us a couple of times, but she doesn't know what happened. Mrs. Acres promised not to upset my parents. If my dad learned of the attack, he may insist I come home. Hopefully, I can make it past August. Then, it will be too late to safely abort the pregnancy.

Mom tells people I'm staying with friends on Qualla Boundary to work in a volunteer program, which requires long hours. When summer's over, she'll figure out another story. I'm sad that she has to fib.

Hannah has told me over and over that forgiveness leads to a peaceful mind, but I can't help despising the awful boy that changed my parents... and me!

One day, dad and Bogey surprise me with a visit, and the conversation goes well.

"We've been trail riding a lot... just dad and me... and I'm riding old Thunder now." My little brother boasts of his new accomplishment.

"Not long ago, that horse was too spirited for him to handle." Smiling, dad verifies Bogey's statement, but my father looks very tired.

Are those new wrinkles on his forehead and between his eyes?

We chat about the weather, the other horses, everything except the obvious… my baby. Dad even lightly embraces me when they leave. Yet, I think it would be a stretch to say he's proud of me for standing up for myself.

Sunday at St. Teresa of Avila Church, Joey Paul asks me to go with him to a movie.

What? Why now?

"Hurry, Nikki, we'll be late. My mother's preparing food." Laura bails me out of an uncomfortable moment.

"Sorry, Joey Paul, gotta run!"

Her mom *is* cooking a meal for us at their house but later today.

In the late afternoon, we drive into town and discover my parents and brother are invited to dinner, too. Surprisingly, we all get along. The aroma of good food, and the soft, classical music that Mrs. Acres chose provides a calming atmosphere.

The delicious hors d'oeuvres of tiny shrimp and basil cream cheese crackers compliment the main course of baked haddock, fresh green beans with pearl onions, and buttered corn muffins.

"Today is Laura's birthday!" Mrs. Acres gestures upward with her hands.

"Why didn't you tell me?" I turn toward my temporary housemate.

"I get embarrassed when people make a fuss." Shyly,

Laura gazes at the floor, and I realize that my voice-of-reason, all-knowing friend is human after all.

Everyone has their fill, and when the last morsel of food disappears from our plates, Laura's mom brings in a homemade chocolate-on-chocolate birthday cake with eighteen flaming candles. Two scoops of coconut ice cream served in fancy little crystal dishes complete the celebration.

Laura's dad takes pictures as she blows out the fiery tapers, and we dive in. Bogey, my dad, and Mr. Acres eat two pieces of cake each.

Dad glances at me and his face lights up. For one tiny second, I see the happy father of my childhood. Still, not fully trusting his sincerity, my eyelids quiver at the thought of his demanding words just a few weeks ago.

* * * *

Monday morning, the day the Bravehearts are due to arrive home, the house phone rings. A clerk of the court gives me the calendar date for the Loveleigh vs Ryder hearing.

"What?" I'm stunned for a moment until it registers. Since I pressed charges against Randolph Ryder, the clerk says I will have to testify in front of Judge Ashley Cuomo.

I'm shocked to hear that my assailant has pleaded guilty. That means no jury, and only the judge will decide Randolph's sentence.

Laura beams at the news. "It'll be over quickly... your name won't be in the newspaper because you're not eighteen yet, and you drew a woman judge. How *just* is that?"

"It's great! Mom and dad won't find out. Will you go with me? It's next Tuesday."

"Of course, and Hannah and Joe will go, too. It's their house the guy broke into." Laura's mind reasons.

Suddenly, the front door swings open, and a hair-tousled Hannah Braveheart tugs her large blue suitcase into the living room. Pulling two more pieces of luggage, Joe follows in his wrinkled shirt and pants. First, they give me a big hug, and then they embrace Laura.

"There's no place like home." Hannah lets out a big sigh. "That's a long trip… and the interstate traffic… wow! I didn't know that many trucks existed!" She plops down on their brown leather sofa.

"We've decided that Oliver should fly home when he finishes Juilliard. He can donate things that can't be checked on an airplane." Chuckling, Joe shakes his head. He seems to be amused at the amount of stuff a kid needs at college.

"What about his musical instruments?" *What's wrong with me? I don't need to be Oliver's advocate.*

"Oh… well, we'll worry about that when the time comes. He has a few years." Hannah shrugs.

Serious now, Joe looks at me with concern. "Are you okay? I'm so sorry you had to go through that awful ordeal."

"I'm fine, and my doctor says the baby is fine, too. But, if that cougar hadn't shown up, it would've been different." Thinking that the kidnapper probably planned to rape me on the basement floor, I fiddle nervously with my fingers.

"How did the animal get in the house?" Joe scratched his head.

"Well, except for the screen door being smashed from the inside, everything was intact, windows, doors… The police couldn't find how Randolph broke in, either. They said he probably had locksmith's tools."

"You know his name?" Hannah looks at me with lifted eyebrows.

"Uh… yes. Randolph Ryder. Actually, he abducted me once before, but I didn't tell anyone."

Horrified, Joe and Hannah want to hear every detail, but I omit Oliver's name from the story.

"That violent man needs to go to jail for a long time." Frowning, Hannah looks at Joe like she wants him to confirm her statement.

Rubbing his chin, Joe quietly ponders the information. Then, obviously troubled, the mild-mannered chief strides around the room.

"Joe, we need to install stronger locks on all the doors and windows." Hannah's eyes follow her husband until his pacing stops.

Joe Braveheart ignores his wife's suggestion and pounds his fist on the dining room table.

"I know that creep's father! He's Randolph Ryder, Sr. who owns Ryder Locksmith Company in Redmond."

Speechless, Hannah, Laura, and I gaze at each other.

* * * *

At the hearing, I'm relieved to see only a few people: Mr. Wells, who was hired by the Bravehearts to represent us, Randolph, his attorney, and the elder Mr. Ryder.

After I state what happened, Judge Ashley Cuomo peers over her black reading glasses and asks Randolph, Jr. to confirm the account.

He verifies it, and I hear why. He's been in trouble for burglary before. No doubt his attorney has advised him to plead guilty in hopes of leniency.

Randolph explains his actions by fabricating a love story. He describes the break-in as a lovesick yearning that he couldn't control. Meanwhile, the judge taps her fingers impatiently on the courtroom desk.

"Bull…" I glare at the offender and turn to our attorney, but Joe and Hannah are whispering to him.

Mr. Wells seems excited and turns to me. "Is that true? He kidnapped you and attempted rape prior to this incident? Can you prove it?"

I think for a minute. "Yes, the other boy, Horse, was there, also.

"You mean, Howard Cook, the other defendant who has a separate hearing vs the state relating to this case?"

I confirm the name, and my attorney asks the judge for a recess until tomorrow.

* * * *

Back in court the next day, three more people appear: Howard, his attorney, and his dad. After Howard validates my story of the first kidnapping, he testifies that Randolph vowed to get even with me and to teach me a lesson.

Judge Cuomo sentences Randolph to ten years in jail without probation for being a repeat offender, lying to the court, kidnapping, assaulting a minor, resisting arrest, and home invasion. The defendant breaks down, sobbing.

He looks at me as the bailiff takes him away in handcuffs, and for the first time, honest regret shows on his face. "I'm sorry. Forgive me," he pleads.

It will be difficult, but how can anyone refuse to forgive someone who's genuinely sorry? Hannah has reminded me many times that forgiveness is a conscious decision, the key to healing emotionally.

Certainly, I'll try, just like I'll try to forgive the thoughtless person who got me pregnant and turned my life upside down.

At Howard's court date, I testify in his defense for untying me and placing me on the yellow air mattress instead of the cold, hard concrete floor. Citing his first offense and his minor role in the crime, the judge gives Howard three months of probation and three months of community service, consecutively.

"Someone has to sweep out the jail every day." He jokes, but I'm sure he is greatly relieved for such a light sentence.

With both hearings behind me, I concentrate on being well for the baby's sake. I exercise, eat more vegetables and fruit, do deep breathing, and try to remain calm about the big decision: adoption or no adoption.

Oliver keeps his promise. He calls every evening and texts often with brief messages:

Monday: "Met a cool dude. Had a cello duel. Fun."

Wednesday: "Miss you. Writing a song just for you." J

He seems to love his classes and the music ensembles he joined. I'm so glad Judge Cuomo didn't know Oliver witnessed the first kidnapping. She may have ordered him to testify, too.

The following week, Hannah goes with me to an ultrasound appointment. At ten weeks, a baby's gender can be determined.

Trying to convince myself the baby is a girl, I sit in the waiting room and pick at my fingernails. Otherwise, why would the angel name her "Blossom"?

Then, I doubt myself.

Maybe I imagined the Cherokee man, the cat, and the flower.

Was I delusional from being knocked unconscious and only thought I saw Adawehi?

Maybe the flower in the woods was just a flower.

Maybe Kimi Wesa was just a stray cat like Hannah said.

But none of that explains how a bear saved me or how a cougar mysteriously showed up inside the house and attacked Randolph.

"Nicole Loveleigh?" A nurse calls my name and startles me out of my head.

Hannah Braveheart squeezes my hand, and I rise to follow the woman clad in a uniform covered with pictures of cats.

I wish my mom was here, too.

For ten minutes, the technician drags a cold metal wand through gooey jelly over my bare tummy, and trying to recognize something, anything, I watch the monitor intently.

Finally, with a nodding smile, she stands up. "The radiologist will be right in to speak with you about the results."

I hold my breath until the door opens and a tall man glides into the small room.

"Well, congratulations. Your ultrasound shows a perfectly developed baby. Do you want to know the sex, or do you want to be surprised?"

"No, I can't wait. Tell me."

"…a perfect baby… girl." The radiologist grins broadly as if declaring a baby's gender was the best part of his job.

"Is Mr. Loveleigh in the waiting room?"

"Uh… no… I'm not married. May I leave now?"

"Yes, and take the ultrasound picture to show your friends

and family." He hands me the shadowy image, and the technician shows me how to read it.

I see a tiny baby! My baby! With a head and arms and legs!

Anxious to share the news with Hannah, I jump into my clothes and dash out of the examining room.

"The baby's a girl."

My kind-hearted friend takes my arm and gently guides me outside.

"What? What's wrong?" I question.

"I know one of the women waiting to be examined."

"Does it matter? I don't know any of them."

"Well, just to be on the safe side..." Hannah studies the baby's image, and her naturally bronze lips curl into a stunning smile. "Let's go celebrate. I have some news, too."

Joyfully, we walk like little kids, hand in hand, swinging our arms, and she drives us to the homemade ice cream store.

I sample pistachio, and sea salt fudge but still select my favorite, coconut almond. It's so creamy and refreshing that I totally forget about her "news."

We chat about clothes, and TV shows. Then, out of the blue, Hannah asks, "Does it make a difference... that the baby is a girl? Are you still considering adoption?"

Why does she ask me such a heavy question when I'm so happy?

"I... I... don't know how to answer that... I'm not sure. There's so much to think about... my education, my parents, my future..."

"All I hear is my, my, my. What about the baby's future, the baby's needs? Don't you think she'll want to be with her birth mother?"

It's the first-time Hannah pushes me to keep Adsila, but practical questions swirl in my brain.

Would mom and dad help me raise her? Where would we live? Would I be able to get a good job? Would my friends laugh and sneer at me? Would the baby's father try to contact me? Would he try to see Adsila?

My mind wanders to that fateful night.

No, I refuse to think about the "monster" who assaulted me and left me to die in the woods. *For all he knew, I was fatally injured.*

How can I ever acknowledge him as a "father?" Fathers shouldn't be violent or aggressive or seek their own pleasure regardless of anyone else's well-being.

Overwhelmed with intensifying thoughts, I weep and the tears flow.

"Have faith, Nikki. Remember, God works in mysterious ways." Hannah comforts me with an affectionate hug. "Believe me, you are a blessed young woman as I am a blessed older woman."

Puzzled, I gaze into her sparkling brown eyes.

"I'm pregnant, too… about three months… with a baby girl."

Chapter Eleven – The Airport

Did I hear her right?

"Really?" I swipe the palms of my hands over my tear-stained cheeks.

"Yes, look." Hannah hands me the ultrasound picture of her baby. "Joe and I have named her Tuwa, the Cherokee word for earth."

"I waited to tell you so we could celebrate together." Her face blooms like a spring flower when we compare the images.

Reflecting on how much Hannah Braveheart has changed me, I hug this Cherokee lady who saved me from making the worse decision of my life: abortion. Hannah's determination, confidence, and courage has inspired me to take control of my circumstances. If only I can decide what is best for the baby and me in the long run, my torment will end.

Hannah looks at me tenderly. "Our babies will be spirit sisters," she says.

She implies that our girls will grow up together, and I can't summon the words to agree with her statement.

* * * *

To keep busy on Cherokee land, I help the elderly with their chores, assist at the local day care for young children, and tutor older kids in English. Helping others keeps me from wallowing in self-pity. When I'm greeted with smiling faces, I don't think about my pregnancy or how I got this way.

In view of our upcoming births, Hannah plows ahead with my home schooling, and we buckle down in the mornings before our volunteer work. I breeze through my classes; English IV, Civics, Psychology, and Cherokee I, as an elective. However, I really miss interacting with my friends.

August has ended, and Labor Day approaches.

This morning, I step into my jeans and tug, but the two sides of the zipper refuse to meet. Accepting the inevitable, I glide downstairs in a free-flowing, tropically-flowered muumuu. I don't care. Twelve weeks have passed, and I'm filled with joy; it's too late for a safe abortion.

At breakfast, Hannah confesses her skirts won't button either and suggests we need to shop for something new to wear. We look down at our bulging tummies and laugh.

"If you want to ride to Asheville, we can check out the boutiques." Her eyes gleam with unexplained excitement.

"Why Asheville?" I wonder if she has another reason to go there.

"For a surprise… let's leave it at that." She's delightfully secretive, so I don't press for an answer.

Early the next day, Hannah and I drive for an hour to an outlet mall. I try on dress after dress with a specific look in mind; one that's loose yet not maternal. Maybe an empire waistline, something I can wear for the next couple of months.

Hannah wants professional-looking clothing that can be worn day or night.

We keep several outfits in mind, just in case the perfect dress isn't found. Then, at the last boutique, a navy-blue chiffon with a V-neck, little cap sleeves, and a form-fitting high waist jumps out at me. A snowflake design embeds the fabric like tiny stars hiding in a night sky, and around the bottom of the A-line skirt, two rows of soft turquoise material magically blend into the sheer, lined chiffon.

Hannah tries on a self-belting, red silk, sleeveless dress, which complements her smooth brown skin, and I pull the navy garment over my head in the next dressing room.

"This is it!" Hannah exclaims through the wall of our enclosures.

"Let me see."

Hearing the door of her dressing room open, I step out of mine.

Hannah's eyes light up, and she confirms my choice. "Fantastic! I love it! That dress is perfect for you."

"And I love the red one on you."

"We'll look so put-together at the Labor Day concert." Hannah grins.

"We're still going?"

"Of course, now hurry and get changed. We have one more stop."

After we purchase our new dresses, Hannah drives the opposite way from home.

I see a sign: Asheville Airport. My heart flipflops.

"Why are we here?"

She won't say, yet her eyes sparkle with anticipation.

The more excited she gets, the more anxious I become. Is it what I'm hoping?

We park and hurry inside.

Wheeling their luggage behind them, deplaning passengers trickle into the terminal of the small airport.

I search the sea of faces from about 100 feet and spot him first.

"Oliver!" I scream and wave my arms.

Hannah and I take turns hugging him. The poor guy will probably have bruises.

He's more muscular than I remember, and taller. His thick, black hair falls below his ears, and those sharp dark eyes pierce my heart. I can't stop staring at him, and he gazes at me until I shyly tuck my head.

"Okay, okay… let's get going. It'll be dark soon." Hannah hurries us toward the exit.

On the way home, Oliver tells us about Juilliard, his classes, and New York City. He asks about my health, happenings on the reservation, and the hearings for Randolph and Howard.

We update him on the details and reveal the results of my ultrasound, which I've been saving to show him. He nods at the image, and I detect a slight smile on his smooth, copper lips.

Then, Hannah breaks the news of *her* pregnancy, and Oliver beams with delight.

When I turn to face him, he glances over the seat at my puffy abdomen.

I shift to avert his attention. "So, are you still playing the cello at the Labor Day concert?"

"Yes, I'll practice with the other musicians tonight and tomorrow… and on Sunday I'll play the school's cello… just for you." He flashes his perfect white teeth.

* * * *

At home, Hannah keeps us apart by sending Oliver and me in different directions. On Saturday morning, he helps in the community garden, and I clean house for an elderly couple on the opposite side of Qualla Boundary. We have no time to talk or to work on our combined songs, and in the evening, he and the band get together.

Late Sunday afternoon, the day of the concert, Oliver leaves to set up his instrument and check the sound.

"See you there." He leans down and pecks me on the cheek.

My heart leaps, my eyelashes flutter, and my head bobs up and down.

That evening, Laura accompanies me and the Bravehearts to the performance.

Hannah wears her new red dress proudly, and I feel stylish in my navy chiffon, which hides my condition very well. Although, I keep my arms folded over my stomach just in case.

The large outdoor amphitheater fills quickly. Music by the Qualla Boundary Band and Choir brings tourist and a few local people from outside Cherokee land, as well.

To my surprise, mom, dad, and Bogey sit about eight rows above us. Mom waves and blows a kiss; my father holds up the palm of one hand; Bogey just snickers.

I had told mom about the concert, but I didn't think my parents would actually attend.

Glancing around, I spot Wolfie and a preppy-looking young lady in a belted khaki skirt who must be his college girlfriend. I guess they're back together. Wolfie seems nice, though a little self-absorbed. "Full of himself," my grand-mother would say. *I hope he doesn't see me.*

The musicians and choir members walk onto the field and take their positions on the portable stage. A hush falls over the crowd as Oliver begins a song from the "Lion King" with a cello solo. I fix my eyes on him, concentrate on the melody, and savor every note in the repeating chorus.

For nearly two hours, the ensemble of musicians plays classic compositions like "Waltz of the Flowers" and "Fur Elise." The choir sings "Old Man River" and other famil-iar songs, but near the end of the concert, the conductor announces Oliver will play and sing his original tune entitled "Nicole to the Ninth."

Oh, my gosh, he named it after me.

Slightly embarrassed, I sweep my eyes across the rows of seats and imagine people grinning. When I glance behind me, my mom stares blankly, and my dad glares boldly. Bogey, of course, giggles.

Joe and Hannah smile and blink their big, brown eyes in approval. Laura nods and lifts one eyebrow like she sus-pected something between Oliver and me all along.

Focusing on the words and music of Oliver's song, I ignore everyone else. I listen to his smooth, confident voice and the mellow sound of his cello and enjoy the happiest day of my life.

About halfway through the solo, Oliver glances up for a second. His eyes meet mine, and an undeniable spark ignites between us. I tremble.

Can it be that he likes me as much as I like him?

At the conclusion of his song, the audience stands up and applauds wildly. Realizing that it's not only me who thinks

Oliver is super talented, I join the crowd by clapping until my hands hurt.

After the Cherokee Choir sings an acapella version of "America the Beautiful," the fireworks start with a bang. Pop… pop… pop! Red, white, and blue streamers shoot into the sky and explode into a multitude of bright stars.

My heart, too, sky-rockets when Oliver joins us and pats my hand affectionately. He leans close and whispers, "I like your dress. You look pretty."

* * * *

The next day, Oliver hurries to catch an early morning flight back to New York City. Quickly saying good-bye, with no touching or pecks on the cheek, he leaves for almost three months.

"I'll see you at Thanksgiving." His serious expression lacks the tender manner of yesterday.

Hannah and Joe drive Oliver to the airport in Ashville while I stay home to catch up on my homework. Although, it's hard to get anything done.

Last night lingers in my mind, and I wonder if Oliver acted out of kindness for an "unfortunate" girl. Would he write and perform music for a pitiful, pregnant person? Yes, I think so. Would he kiss a sad girl on the cheek to comfort her? Would he tell her she looks pretty? Yes, and yes.

* * * *

For the next few weeks, Hannah and I gain weight equally in our pregnancies. No longer able to fit into any of our clothes, we often shop at the Qualla Boundary thrift store for maternity garments, which have no style whatsoever. Settling on oversized muumuus, I tolerate my condition in the tent-like dresses. On the other hand, as a public figure in the community, Hannah struggles to appear neat and business-like in casual clothes.

One day, Laura and her mom pick me up to go shopping. My eyes dart to the front passenger who grins sheepishly. Does my mother feel guilty for her dwindling visits, or does she feel empathy for her seventeen-year-old pregnant daughter? I'm sure it's difficult for her to see me in this condition.

"Mom, I'm glad you could come shopping with us." Climbing into the back seat with Laura, I fold my arms over my protruding tummy.

"Mrs. Acres invited me... last night." My mother seems to apologize for not giving me advanced notice. "Your dad doesn't know I'm here. He..."

I interrupt her explanation. "It's fine, mom. Dad's discontent about the baby is his problem, not mine."

"He doesn't go horseback riding with his friends any more. He's afraid they'll tease him for grandfathering a mixed-breed child." Mom spews her words matter-of-factly.

Cringing at her prejudiced statement, I suddenly feel sick to my stomach, raise my voice, and spit out my response.

"First, no one knows the father's identity, least of all me. And second, dad doesn't have to be a grandfather. I'll never come home again, if that's what he wants."

"I'm sorry, Nikki. Maybe I shouldn't have come." She lowers her head.

"Mom, it's okay. I shouldn't have yelled, but this pregnancy is not my fault... and I'm not taking the blame. We'll just have to work through this one day at a time." I try to smooth my mother's hurt feelings.

She turns and looks at me through teary eyes. "Your father thinks Oliver is responsible because of the song he wrote. You know, "Nicole to the Ninth," like the ninth month."

"For the last time… Oliver Rainchild is *not* the father of my baby. He wasn't even at the pool party that night. He's just a sweet guy trying to be supportive of… a rape victim. He has a *heart*!" Loudly, I emphasize the word heart.

For the rest of the drive, everyone sits quietly, but my mind won't shut up. I think of adoption versus keeping little Addie, and of Oliver's possible role in our future. Somehow, my plans to become Professor Nicole Loveleigh fall away, and my baby's welfare dominates my thoughts.

I'm not in a shopping mood today, but two useful items pop up at a re-purposed accessory store: a long lacy vest to conceal my baby bulge, and a blue pashmina to drape over my shoulders like a shawl.

On the return home, my mother asks to be dropped off first, in order to prepare dinner.

I hope dad is tending the horses and doesn't see me?

We feign a hug, and as soon as she steps away from the car, my cell phone rings.

O-o-o-o-ga!

While waving good-bye, I look down and recognize Carly's number. Slowly, I touch the "talk" button, without speaking. *Do I really want to talk to her?*

Chapter Twelve – The Truth

"Nikki? Hello? Can you hear me?" My hesitation seems to put Carly on edge.

"Yes, hello. How are you, Carly?" I speak as pleasantly as I can.

"Why haven't you answered my texts? Where are you? Someone heard you're in Florida, and someone else saw you on Cherokee land." Carly sounds baffled.

"Actually…" I pause to gather my story. "I went to see my grandparents in Florida, but now I'm visiting friends in Qualla Boundary… you know, since I met some kids at vacation bible school this summer. Sorry, I didn't answer your texts." My excuse sounds vague; I'm such a bad liar.

"Are you coming back to school? I don't know what to tell people."

"Carly, everything is great, but I can't talk right now. I'll call you soon." My eyelids flutter nervously, and I tap the "end call" button.

Moaning to Mrs. Acres and Laura, my eyes well up with tears. "What am I supposed to say to people?"

My all-knowing friend speaks first. "I see three choices.

One, live up to the truth... own it and get it over with. Two, say nothing... talk to no one, ever again. Three, continue to lie for the rest of your life about the baby."

Sniveling like a toddler whose freedom has been limited, I weigh the choices. "I can't lie forever..." Sniff, sniff. "... and it would be impossible not to talk to my friends, and I can't tell the truth... can I?" Sniff.

Laura's mom stops the car in front of the Braveheart's house. "You may find peace of mind if *you* reveal your condition... think about it. Even though you're completely innocent, someone else was there, and he could distort the truth." She speaks softly, and her words float like soap bubbles.

Mrs. Acres is a kind and gentle woman, whereas her daughter expresses herself determinedly.

"Yes, would you rather tell the facts, or let *him* whisper it his way?" Laura's green eyes pierce deeply into my soul. "Apparently, the culprit already started a rumor that you were "overly-friendly" in the woods. You need to set people straight!"

"What about my father and our family name? If I say I'm pregnant, people will talk and judge. But, if I put the baby up for adoption, maybe no one will ever find out."

"Nikki, this is your life *and* your baby's life. No one else matters, no one." Mrs. Acres emphasizes "no one."

"Talk it over with Hannah," Laura advises.

The voice of reason is very persuasive, and Laura's mom hits a cord when she says "your baby's life." *I did promise myself to protect Adsila.*

Walking into the house, my spirits lift immediately. Hannah sings in the kitchen while she prepares the evening meal for Joe, herself, and me. The aroma of made-from-scratch cornbread, fresh-caught rainbow trout, home-grown yellow squash and ramps teases my taste buds and puts a smile on my face. The Bravehearts make an effort to eat a natural diet, and since living here, I appreciate simple, unprocessed food more than ever.

Long ago, before any European influence, the Cherokee were hunter-gatherers. They hunted deer, birds, fish, and rabbits and gathered greens, nuts, wild leeks, known as ramps, and berries. Their staples—corn, squash, and beans—named "the three sisters" were grown in gardens.

Today, with wild game not as bountiful and plant gatherings not as abundant, some families load up on canned food, or boxed goods for convenience... definitely, not as fresh.

* * * *

After dinner, Hannah and I relax in the white rockers on the front porch, and Joe watches football on TV. The cool autumn evening clears my thoughts, and I raise the subject of possibly revealing my condition to my friends.

"Logically, it's my only choice, especially if I continue to live in this town. People will find out sooner or later." I reason.

"I've thought about it a lot..." Hannah hesitates. "But it has to be your decision. A few people will be cruel, and you'll have to expect that."

Hannah's gentle brown eyes probe mine. "Does this mean you're keeping little Addie?"

"No, I don't know what it means... I haven't decided yet. I'm just thinking out loud." Rocking forward, I launch my chubby self out of the chair, shuffle through the living room, and climb the stairs with labored breath.

Why can't I make a definite choice about the baby? What's wrong with me?

The next morning, Hannah greets me with resolve. "We're going to St. Teresa of Avila today to pray for the right words for you to tell your friends."

Even though I haven't fully chosen to disclose my pregnancy, I agree to go. Being inside the church comforts me, and a feeling of love, peace, and joy comes over me.

The stained-glass windows depicting the holy family bathe the sanctuary in colored light and envelop the room in a spiritual cocoon. A forgiving, larger-than-life replica of Jesus on the cross overlooks a white linen-covered altar, and the life-size statue of Mother Mary spreads love throughout the entire space.

Over the past weeks, Hannah has shared some of the traditions of the Catholic Church like praying the rosary and partaking of the Eucharist at every mass. I *have* made one important decision: to become Catholic after the baby's born. It just feels right.

Hannah says history traces the Catholic popes back to Saint Peter, the first pope, who founded the first Christian church that is the Catholic Church today.

Today, Hannah and I kneel before the tabernacle, rosaries in hand, and I experience a quiet mind. Glancing at the Blessed Virgin's statue, I hear Hannah whisper.

"Mary likes to untie knots."

Immediately, silent words arise in my head. "Don't worry. Everything will be all right."

Surely, Mary senses the confusion and doubt that plagues me. So, with joy in my heart, I decide to let go, to let Mother Mary loosen this tangled rope around my neck.

We stand up, make the sign of the cross, and bow with

respect before turning to leave. Lowering my eyes, I hope to avoid contact or conversation with people entering the church.

"Hello." Hannah greets a lady coming down the aisle.

Because Hannah serves in the healing ministry, the woman stops to tell her about a parishioner who needs prays.

I continue walking slowly, head down, while they pray together.

"Nikki Loveleigh?" A male voice startles me, and spontaneously, I glance up.

No! Why is it always him?

"Joey Paul." I acknowledge the boy I used to be gaga over.

"I keep seeing you here, even though you say you aren't Catholic." Amused, he chuckles.

"Well, I'm happy to inform you that I may join soon." Proudly, I hold my head high until I notice him gawking at my swollen stomach.

Why didn't I wear my shawl?

"Uh... my family is here to pray for my aunt." He tries to overcome the awkward moment.

"Joey Paul, sit with me for a minute." Taking him by the hand, I lead him to the middle of a pew.

I don't know... the timing is right. The church seems like the right place, and I feel confident that Mother Mary has my back.

"I'm pregnant... Do you remember, in May, Charlie Quinn's pool party ended suddenly when his parents came home unexpectedly?" Stunned, he nods, and I continue.

"All the kids ran into the woods. I fell into a ravine, hit a tree or a rock, and was knocked out. When I woke up the next morning, the only evidence of someone else being there was a boy's shoe and footprints. Then, weeks later, a doctor tells me… this." Gently, I rub my hand over my baby bump and wait for Joey Paul to say something.

"Oh, my God, Nikki… someone attacked you! I'm so sorry… maybe if I hadn't left early…" He sounds genuinely upset.

"I've heard rumblings about you and a guy in the woods, but I didn't believe it." Joey Paul shakes his head in disbelief.

"Well, trust me… there was no 'guy.'" I flash a set of quotation marks in the air with my fingers. "At least, none that I saw." I surprise myself at how easily I can talk to Joey Paul.

"What are you going to do?"

"For the moment, my dad makes it uncomfortable for me to live at home, so I'm staying with the Bravehearts. Hannah does home-schooling." I pause and study his sympathetic expression, his suntanned face, and his true-blue eyes. Some lucky girl will have a great boyfriend one of these days.

"You're the first one to hear my story, other than Laurie Acres. It was easier to tell you than I imagined." I smile at him. "By the way, why *did* you leave the party so early?"

"I wanted to ask you to slow dance, but you were having fun with your friends." Frown lines gather between his eyes. "And, I'm not much of a swimmer or a drinker."

"Oh." I stand up to join Hannah as she departs from the church.

"Is it okay to phone or text you some time… to see how you are?"

"It's okay… but please, let me tell people about the baby in my own time." I gaze at him a moment, sadly imagining what could have been.

Hannah doesn't say anything but gives me a questioning glance.

"I felt compelled to tell him." Quietly, I speak as we walk. "I'm sure the Blessed Virgin interceded; the right words just came to me." I look over my shoulder and Joey Paul still watches as we leave the church.

"I recognize him as Mrs. Haute's son, but how do you know him? Isn't he older?"

"I've had a crush on Joey Paul since I was in the eighth grade and he was in the ninth. But, we never dated... and now we're just friends."

On the way home, I give thanks that the worry of how to tell people is off my shoulders. Just spitting out the truth seems like the best way.

"Does this mean you'll tell your other friends about the baby?" Hannah Braveheart, my good friend and teacher, searches my face for an answer.

I shrug.

Will it be as easy to reveal my secret next time?

* * * *

The next day, I gather my courage to invite Carly to the Braveheart's house after school. When I hear her old yellow jeep barreling down the road, I peer out the window as it screeches to a stop in a cloud of dust.

Hannah is running errands for home bound elders, so I yell for Carly to come upstairs.

She bursts into the room in a chatty whirlwind, which quickly turns to silence. Carly's face turns pale at the sight of me sitting on the bed with my tummy extended.

"What the hell?" Carly's expression contorts like something totally unimaginable is in front of her.

I state the facts like I did with Joey Paul. It goes smoothly, and I feel okay. It's over. She can tell everyone else.

Carly bawls. She cries uncontrollably, probably more than I did when I first found out. She hugs me and sobs some more. "Are you absolutely sure???" she moans.

"Carly, Carly… it's okay. It's not the end of the world." Funny, I console her.

"It's the end… of… our… innocence!" She bawls louder. "I can't believe this! How could somebody do this to you? I hate him! … to be raped by someone you don't even know who…" Carly's mood goes from denial to outrage.

I offer her a tissue, and she honks her nose like a sailor.

"Did you call the police?" Now, she's defensive, like how-can-we-fix this.

"No, I didn't even know I'd been raped until a month later when I missed my period." Sadly, I glance out the window, realizing Carly is right; the time of my youthful virtue is over.

"Besides, my father accused me of lying, and my mother was almost paralyzed with panic. I had no evidence except a shoe that could've been lost by anyone at any time. I thought the police wouldn't believe me either."

After Carly rants and raves some more, she asks the big question. "Will you keep the baby or put it up for adoption?"

"I haven't decided. It's the hardest thing I've ever had to think about." I gaze at my young friend, and she nods her head in agreement.

I ask her to discreetly disclose my pregnancy to my close friends, and we continue to talk until Hannah and Joe come home.

Solemnly, hand in hand, Carly and I walk downstairs and greet the Bravehearts. They are quietly cordial and seem to sense the reason Carly is here.

Do they think revealing the truth is a step toward keeping the baby? Do I?

As Carly's jeep pulls away, more thoughtfully than when it arrived, I wave good-bye and wonder... have I accepted motherhood?

O-o-o-o-ga! O-o-o-o-ga!

Jumping out of my skin, I question my sanity.

Really? Why haven't I changed this obnoxious ringtone?

Chapter Thirteen – Lost

"Hello, Joey Paul."

My past "crush" has called to express his concern for me.

"I'm okay. Thanks for your understanding and support." My calmness amazes me.

A few months ago, I would've floated on cloud nine and fumbled my words if he had called. Funny how situations develop, feelings change, and new attitudes begin.

Is this what growing up feels like?

* * * *

October has come and gone with Oliver's calls and texts becoming less frequent. I understand he's busy with school, but I miss his voice and our midnight talking sessions. Sometimes, I fall asleep holding my new smart phone, which mom so graciously bought for me.

My new ringtone plays the chorus from Oliver's song, "Nicole to the Ninth." The lines offer me hope for the future, and I pray they're not random words strung together or worse, sympathetic lyrics:

Nicole, my sweet one, never a faint one,
Oh, my love, come sing today.
Nicole, my friend now, never bend some,
Come be with me always.

Nevertheless, the phrase "… my friend now, never bend some" causes me to wonder about myself. Will my feelings for Oliver fade like my infatuations with Joey Paul and Wolfie?

Since our conversation at church, Joey Paul calls or texts every day. Very often, when you lose something, you gain something else. Now, I see him as a good friend or a big brother rather than a potential boyfriend.

Joey Paul has offered to investigate the "shoe," but I prefer not to know the truth, to pretend my baby was conceived by miraculous circumstances rather than aggression, lust, and selfishness.

My close friends, Carly, Laurie, Charlie, and Gary visit often with little gifts like magazines, blizzards, MP3s of new tunes, or sample cosmetics from our downtown department store.

Today, Carly surprises me and brings an old DVD of *Live in Amsterdam* by Tina Turner, my music idol. We sing and dance to Tina's choreographed steps and fall down on the bed, laughing. She's more into Katy Perry, but she humors me. Carly lifts my spirits, and I will miss her silly ways when she goes skiing with her parents this month.

Thanksgiving approaches with all the usual holiday expectations. Among them, shopping, cooking, and family reunions top the discussions in the Braveheart house. With high hopes, I anticipate Oliver's first homecoming since September's concert, but being six months pregnant, I worry my unattractiveness will turn him away.

Lying in bed one night with my phone close by, "Nicole to the Ninth," interrupts my half-asleep state.

"Hello!" I force myself to sound bright and cheery.

"Hi, Nikki. How are you?" Oliver's voice sounds a little reserved.

"Missing you and counting the days until Thanksgiving." I put my whole heart into my answer.

"That's why I'm calling… I've been invited to go skiing. So, I'm not coming home until Christmas break, which is only two weeks after Thanksgiving." His tone is apologetic.

"But… I miss you, too, and can't wait to see that healthy glow that comes with carrying a baby." His words are upbeat now.

I feign happiness for his skiing trip, but negativity creeps into my mind.

Yeah, of course! What fun would it be watching a big-stomached woman eat Thanksgiving dinner?

"Have fun and be safe." I hold back a million tears. "Gotta go… bye." I hang up quickly before my voice quivers.

The next morning, two days before Thanksgiving, chilly air awakens me, and I linger under the warm covers. After building up enough courage to roll back the blanket, I gaze out the window at Hannah's frost-tipped garden. Large orange pumpkins, plump winter squash, and the beefy sweet potatoes that lounge beneath rich soil leisurely await their purpose. Soon, ovens across Qualla Boundary will bake delicious pies, hearty casseroles, and traditional American Indian dishes.

At breakfast, Hannah and Joe greet me with sympathetic eyes, and I know Oliver has called them, also.

"Yes, I know. Oliver's going skiing on his Thanksgiving

break." Putting on a happy face, I acknowledge the news and add a cheerful idea.

"With the extra two weeks until his homecoming, lets surprise him with a house full of Christmas decorations. I'll make miniature trees out of boxwood for each little table and cover them with colorful ornaments."

"I'll chop a tall cedar tree for the living room, and honor it with bright lights." Showing his eagerness to make this year special with a tree that's sacred to the Cherokee, Joe winks. After all, he and Hannah have something to celebrate. Their baby girl, Tuwa, will be born in early spring.

"I'll bake Oliver's favorite Christmas goodies: banana-merengue pie, oatmeal-cranberry cookies, and chocolate cupcakes with red and green icing." Hannah's eyes sparkle with love.

The Braveheart's enthusiasm for Christmas almost puts me into a good mood.

After I wolf down a stack of Hannah's famous blueberry pancakes drenched in butter and whipped cream, I venture outside to sample the crisp fall air. Breathing in and out rhythmically, as my doctor taught me, I wander toward the woods. Even though the sun shines bright and cheery, the wind sways the trees and hypnotizes me back into an adverse state of mind.

Why would Oliver want to be with me for Thanksgiving? He's never said we're "together" or "dating" or anything. It's just me... assuming. My fantasy. Me, thinking he likes me because of a peck on the cheek and a song he wrote. Big deal. It's just a tune that came into his head. What a starry-eyed romantic I am.

How could Oliver fall for a girl who's pregnant with another man's baby? Who could do that?

I feel deserted, sorry for myself. My own father hates me. My mother only pacifies me, and my brother treats me like I'm a big joke. I haven't seen or heard anything from Adawehi or Kimi Wesa for weeks.

Maybe if I go deeper into the woods, my Cherokee angel will appear.

Wondering if the flower still blooms in the ravine, I trample through bushes and weeds and stumble over rocks and roots. It would be west of here. I just have to walk in the opposite way of the sun.

Why didn't I bring my phone? Not that it would work out here anyway.

The dense forest sparkles with drops of melting frost, but nothing looks familiar. Entering from Cherokee land, the trees are closer together like matchsticks in a box. The land lies flat, unlike the rough terrain behind my house.

I listen for the sounds of rushing river water; I sniff the air for the scent of cinnamon; I gaze past the trees for familiar pathways. Nothing. *Maybe I should just go home.*

Uneasy now, I turn around and start walking in the direction that I believe to be the location of Joe and Hannah's house.

Minutes pass, and the scream of an angry animal pierces my eardrums. At first, I hope Adawehi will appear and rescue me, but the beast bellows again, closer this time.

I walk faster, and the unfamiliar territory becomes hilly. *Surely, this is not the way.*

Turning sharp, I trip over kudzu vines and tumble head over heels into a shallow gully. My abdomen aches, my right shoulder twinges, and my ankle throbs.

In a failed attempt to stand up, I face facts: my painful ankle may be broken, and a wild animal may eat me for lunch. Sobbing quietly, I curl into a fetal position and hide among the dried leaves. *I feel so stupid. Why did I come out here?*

Lying still, I listen for the angry animal but only hear the chatter of the forest.

Bluejays and mocking birds vie for nesting territory while the faint chirp of a predator hawk communicates a willingness to wait for eggs or baby birds. *Is the untamed creature waiting for me? Did Adawehi make it go away?*

Soon, my ears tune to a different sound.

A human voice pleads in the distance. "Nikki... Nikki? Call out if you can hear us?"

Is that Joe Braveheart?

"Nikki... Nikki? Where are you?" Louder... more distinct. Closer.

Hannah?

Then the booming male voices of Charlie and Gary cry out. "Nikki Loveleigh!"

"Here... here." The feeble words barely escape my parched throat.

Trying harder, I muster some oomph. "Here! Over here!"

Carefully, the team of rescuers pulls me from the leaf grave and surrounds me with love. Hannah wipes my dirt-splattered face; Joe assesses my swollen ankle; Charlie and Gary assemble a make-shift carrier with blankets from their backpacks.

"I can't believe you looked for me. How did you find me?" Weak, but grateful, I realize how lucky I am to have such great friends.

"That cat... the stray..." Hannah pauses.

"What cat?"

Do I dare think it was Kimi Wesa?

Joe motions with his hands. "The big one that hangs around the house. It ran back and forth toward the forest, yowling."

"When the guys came for a visit, they saw the cat acting strangely. So, after Hannah and I realized you'd been gone since breakfast, we thought we'd better follow the cat…"

"Joe, did you hear the wild animal screams?"

"It was just a peacock." He avoids my gaze and continues bandaging my ankle.

Hannah fusses over me as the guys lift me onto the carrier. "Just look at all these leaves." Lovingly, she picks them off my clothes one by one.

Sunbeams streak through the canopy of trees, and I notice Hannah's face glowing with the healthy radiance that Oliver talked about. *I hope I have a glow.*

"The cat led us straight to you." With tousled hair and tenderness in his eyes, Charlie gazes at me. "Is it yours?"

My orange-haired friend and I had been close ever since my sophomore year. Charlie worked in the snack bar at school, and every day, my hardest decision was deciding which crackers to buy. Once, when I'd finally made my selection, he said, "I hope you've found some 'nabs' you like." I thought that was the funniest thing I'd ever heard. We laughed and laughed.

"It's… Kimi." My soft voice exposes my exhaustion. "Where is… she now?" I'm barely able to form the words.

"Just a minute ago, she was watching from that tree." Gary points to a massive white oak.

I glance up, but she's gone.

Adawehi and Kimi Wesa *do* care. They haven't abandoned me.

My friends take turns carrying me, and soon the house is in sight.

"You were only about a half mile from home." Joe directs my gaze with a gesture.

I want to go inside and lie down on my bed. However, Hannah insists on driving me to the ER for my ankle and other possible injuries. I protest, but she won't say more; she keeps leading the guys to her SUV.

To my horror, when I'm transferred from the carrier to the car, I notice blood stains on the blankets. "What is that?" I scream with the new-found energy that panic brings. "My baby, my baby… is she all right?"

"Nikki, stay calm. It's the best thing you can do until we get to the hospital. Breathe slowly and evenly, and you and your baby will be fine." Hannah advises me like a nurse.

I trust her. So, I follow her instructions and try not to worry.

In the emergency room, doctors and nurses swarm like bees. With an ultrasound, they see a slight tear in the placenta has caused the bleeding. My doctor admits me into the hospital for complete bed rest to prevent more separation.

After the medical staff determines my pregnancy is stable, they agree my ankle and my shoulder are only badly bruised.

Hannah and Joe promise not to tell Oliver. I don't want to interfere with his plans, not that he would call them off, or should he, for that matter.

The hospital keeps me a few days, through Thanksgiving, but Hannah, my mom, and my friends bring more food than an army can eat. Even Joey Paul delivers an apple pie his mom made, which I share with my nurses.

While I was flat on my back, Carly travelled with her

parents to Lake Tahoe to ski on the snow-covered mountains of Heavenly, California. When she returned and visited me at the Braveheart's house, she brought devastating news.

"I saw Oliver Rainchild. He and a girl were skiing on the beginner slopes."

My jaw drops to the floor, but I manage to recover before Carly detects my dismay. "Oh… what a small world." I keep my welling eyes glued to the fashion magazine she gave me.

Our conversation remains casual until Carly looks at me empathetically and says I should rest.

Silently, I welcome her departure.

The image of Oliver and a girl at Lake Tahoe overwhelms me. My foolish daydreams of him sharing a life with me and Addie are completely shattered. My sliver of hope vanishes.

How naïve can I be?

Reality sets in, and adoption appears to be the only answer that makes sense for me and the baby.

How could I have hoped Oliver would help me raise this child?

Tears stream.

But wait… didn't I want a career anyway? Mother Mary, pray for me. I don't know what I want.

I burrow my wet face into the bed pillow until Hannah calls "dinner time."

Chapter Fourteen – Snowy Moon

December arrives.

I've always loved the last month on the calendar for its crisp air, the possibility of snow, my birthday, and a joyful Christmas spirit everywhere… except for this year.

This year, I dislike December. I wish I could skip it altogether. The sky is an ugly gray, and gloom is everywhere. I've lost my perceived relationship with Oliver, and I've been confined to my bed for days.

Finally, my obstetrician declares the placenta has healed, and the baby is out of danger. He recommends mild exercise such as walking, since I've been inactive for a while, and that makes me happy.

My spirit craves the great outdoors, to see the forest, to smell the trees, but my courage needs to reboot. So, when Gary calls, I ask him to walk with me along the edge of the woods.

As my friend and I leave the house, Hannah says Oliver will fly into Asheville today and catch a shuttle home. I shrug nonchalantly and twist my face into a who-cares-look.

Hannah looks puzzled, and her mouth gapes open. She doesn't know I've avoided his calls since Thanksgiving.

Ignoring the late-night rings and his daily texts has summoned all my will power. I need to distance myself from Oliver. If I don't, my crush on him will crush *me*.

Oliver's shuttle van pulls up at the same time as Gary and I return from our stroll. His face droops at the sight of my tow-headed friend holding my hand, albeit in a protective, brotherly way. Or, maybe Oliver is shocked to see my seventh month belly. I don't care.

Anyway, we don't talk. Gary leaves, and I waddle up the stairs to my room.

At dinner, Joe and Hannah and Oliver chat jovially while I stare at my bowl of vegetable soup. Oliver comments on the bare, eight-foot tree in the living room, and Joe explains the delay in stringing it with lights.

"I wanted to wait until everyone could pitch in with the decorations."

"Well, Nikki and I will have to get busy." Oliver leans back in his chair and grins at me.

Involuntarily, my eyes glance at him.

How can he look much older and mature? He's been gone only a few weeks.

Shaking my head negatively, I gulp the remainder of my food and escape to the front porch.

Oliver has offered to dry the dishes tonight, so I relax in my favorite rocker and breathe the cool evening air until…

"Hannah said you fell in the forest and were restricted to bedrest." Oliver takes my hand and presses it to his cheek. "Why didn't you answer your phone?"

I jerk my hand away. "What are you doing?"

Oliver seems startled but presses for an answer. "Why didn't anyone tell me about your accident?"

"Hannah and Joe agreed not to say anything. We didn't want to upset your plans with your... with your *skiing*."

He stares at me, dumbfounded. "Are you mad at me for going skiing with my friend Tucker and his family?"

"Of course not." I try to sound convincing.

Wait...

"Did you say "his family"? My eyelids blink nervously.

"Yes, Tucker's mom and dad and his younger sister. Shelby had never skied, so we took turns with her on the beginners run. It was hilarious, falling down so much. I'm not that good of a skier myself."

"Oh..." I realize that I have put myself through needless torture.

Then, I blurt, "Carly saw you skiing at Lake Tahoe."

"Is that what this is all about? Silly girl, you were jealous." He lifts my chin and kisses me lightly on the lips. "You are the only silly girl for me," he whispers.

When Joe ambles onto the porch, I excuse myself and ascend the stairs, slowly. Still blushing from Oliver's confession, I crawl under the bedcovers and close my eyes for a peaceful sleep.

Thank you, Mother Mary. You were right; I shouldn't worry.

The next morning, I hear rumbling and shuffling downstairs.

"What's happening?" I descend one step at a time to guarantee my surefootedness.

"Tree trimming." Oliver laughs and his bronze lips widen over snow-white teeth. "After breakfast, we're digging into these boxes and decorating this huge tree."

I smile at him. Hannah smiles at me, and Joe smiles at Hannah. Peace, love, and joy. Even though, my little miniature trees will have to wait for another year, this Christmas will be the best ever.

After a hardy breakfast of veggie omelets and diced potatoes, we tackle the fragrant cedar. Joe and Oliver string seven cords of LED lights, a number that holds special meaning for the seven clans of the Cherokee.

Oliver drags a chair over for me to decorate the lower half of the tree. He sets out boxes of white feathered doves, angel ornaments, and tiny animal figurines. With each glittering piece, the sacred cedar forms into a beacon of hope for the future.

In between pecks on the cheek, Oliver brings me hot chocolate and Christmas cookies from Hannah's stash. Maybe he's just caught up in the spirit of the season, but his attentiveness dares me to think.

Is he just being nice, or does he want a life with me and little Addie?

Christmas chatter dominates every conversation, and I hear the family plans to attend the Cherokee Lights and Legends Festival this weekend. Oliver can't believe I've never been to Qualla Boundary's holiday festivities. He describes the big bonfire and storytelling that mesmerizes the crowd. I listen attentively; this is who I want to be now.

A few days before Christmas and with Hannah's gift of a red shawl folded across my mid-section, my new family and I arrive at the Cherokee Indian Fair Grounds. The fragrant scent of wood smoke warmly greets us, and colored lights guide us down a wide path to the fun activities.

Face painting, mini-golf, an ice rink, and Santa's house thrill the children, but best of all, a spectacular 30 ft. high spruce brings joy to the celebration with hundreds of twinkling white lights.

Hannah and Joe stop to talk with friends and Oliver and I continue exploring. We stop at a place near the blazing fire, and Oliver explains the tribal tradition of combining Cherokee customs and Christian bible stories.

I listen as an elder chief describes Winter Solstice, a peaceful period during the Christmas season when tribes celebrate family. Their crops have been harvested and preparations for winter are complete. Families relax, feast, and rejoice in being together. It's a time that coincides with Christian families celebrating Christ's birth with love and gift giving.

Oliver and I stroll, hand in hand, along the lighted pathway and notice a group of people gazing into a corral with sheep, goats, a donkey, and a cow. Stepping closer, I look past the rustic fence, past the animals, and stare into a lean-to shed.

Three men dressed like kings admire a baby in a small straw bed. The mother tends to the fussy baby while the father watches over them.

They're real people, and that's a real baby.

Not expecting to see a real-life Nativity scene with Mary, Joseph, and baby Jesus, I study the figures and notice one that doesn't fit. An old Cherokee man kneels behind the baby and looks straight at me.

It's Adawehi! Why is he here?

I panic and fear that the magical time with Oliver will end. My heart throbs. I want to run from reality, from this pregnancy, from whatever the angel says, but then… I hear his voice, his melodic chant, and it calms my mind.

"Ad-sila do-hi. Ni-ki hi-ne-yu. Ol-i-ver a-da-ga-u-e Ni-ki."

Concentrating on Adawehi's words, I'm unaware of Oliver's expression until his statement forces me to look at him.

"They're such a beautiful family." Oliver watches the scene intently, and the reflection of the bonfire illuminates his face. "Family is everything."

Hesitating for a minute, I question him. "Do… you… see the old Indian man?"

Oliver faces me. "I see and hear him. He said, 'Adsila healthy. Nikki keep. Oliver loves Nikki.'"

Wriggling to remove my hand from Oliver's, I remember that Adawehi said he would see me on the Snowy Moon, December. *But I didn't know he would embarrass me!*

Oliver holds tight to my twisting fingers and won't let go. "Nikki, I do love you, more each day. I love Adsila, too… Let's go sit by the tree."

Oliver guides me to an empty bench away from the crowd. He stands in front of me and gets down on one knee. "Nikki Loveleigh, will you marry me?" The soon-to-be nineteen-year-old stares into my astonished face.

When he takes a gold-streaked, turquoise ring from his pocket, my lower lip trembles.

A wide silver band, etched with American Indian symbols, supports the scrollwork that cradles the blue-green gemstone. I've never seen anything so beautiful.

"This ring was attached to my blanket when the Bravehearts found me. We think it's an heirloom that belonged to my ancestors." Oliver's soft tone is reverent of his descendants.

"Oh." Somehow, my one-word response seems inappropriate.

"Nikki?" Oliver prompts for a yes or no answer to his question.

Still, I have questions of my own. "How, when, where... I mean... what about Juilliard?" I shake with unbelief. *Am I dreaming?*

"I've given it a lot of thought. You and Addie can stay with Hannah and Joe until the school year ends. If you agree, we can have a June wedding here on Qualla Boundary. When my classes start again, the three of us can move to New York and begin our lives." He looks at me with love and respect.

I regard him with love and trust. "Okay... yes." My heart pounds with excitement, and my eyelids quiver, in a good way.

Oliver's firm copper lips touch mine, tenderly. "Let's go home."

Back at the Bravehearts' house, Oliver and I announce our plans. Hannah and Joe are ecstatic and agree that the baby and I are welcome, indefinitely.

When I go upstairs to freshen up, Hannah comes in and tells me about a vivid dream. "I dreamed that Tuwa and Adsila grow up to aid other American Indian tribes in becoming sovereign like the Eastern Band of Cherokee Nations. They were on top of a mountain holding legal papers, and hundreds of tribespeople cheered the two women as heroines."

"What would sovereignty mean?" I sit with her on the side of my bed.

"American Indians on reservations would have control over tribal membership, and manage their land's resources of timber, oil, minerals, and water. I believe the dream is a sign that our girls will accomplish great things for all tribes." Hannah smiles. "I didn't want to influence you unfairly, so I waited to tell you the dream after you decided to keep your baby."

Oliver, Hannah, Joe, and I talk for a couple of hours and discuss our wedding, Oliver adopting Adsila, and our move to New York.

After I say goodnight and crawl into bed, I marvel at how situations turn out... how one thing leads to another, like someone plans the circumstances. *God incidents.*

Maybe Hannah and Laura are right. Addie has a destiny to fulfill.

One thing's for sure, I'll be Mrs. Oliver Rainchild, and my baby will be Kachina Adsila Rainchild.

Drifting off to sleep with a smooth face, instead of the usual furrowed brow, I think of the time that Mother Mary's statue held out her arms to comfort me.

She knew my baby would have a caring father figure, just like Joseph cared for her baby.

The next morning, I awake with apprehension and dread the phone call to my parents.

"Mom, let's have lunch."

She says my dad and brother are walking their horses up the mountain, so she invites me to the house.

"You look well and rested. I hope everything's okay after your fall." She pauses. "We... were worried about you."

"We?" I raise an eyebrow and wonder if she includes dad in that "we."

"Yes, your father has a tough exterior, but on the inside, he loves you very much."

"Mother, I've forgiven dad for being harsh, but that's not what I came to talk about." I press my lips together and remember that the best way to deliver news is to spit it out.

"Oliver Rainchild asked me to marry him. Our wedding

will be in June, and he plans on adopting Adsila." I wait for her response, which is slow coming. "Oh, and one more thing… it will be a Catholic wedding with Cherokee traditions."

She glares in disbelief before questions fly. "What about college… and your career? How can he support you and a baby?"

"Please, mom, Oliver's very talented. Already, he has an offer to play cello with the New York Symphony Orchestra when he graduates from Juilliard."

"You'll live in New York?" Tears form in the corners of her eyes.

"Yes, and with many opportunities… college classes, jobs, day care for Addie." I try to soften my announcement.

"But, you're just eighteen this month," she sobs.

"Mom, you were eighteen, and the Blessed Virgin Mary was younger than that. We'll visit often, and you can visit us. I love Oliver, and he loves me and Addie."

After mom digests the news of my marriage, she wishes me a happy birthday for tomorrow, the nineteenth of December, and hands me a gift-wrapped package.

I rip it open, and a white Catholic bible with an angel embossed on the cover delights me.

"How did you know?" I study my mother's hazel eyes.

"Hannah told me you want to convert." At first, she avoids my gaze, then she quizzes me about the difference in bibles.

Briefly, I explain that the Catholic bible has seven extra books in the Old Testament, but the New Testament is the same as the King James version.

Leaving my parent's house with my mom's blessing, I wonder how my father will react to my plans. Legally, he can do nothing. Turning eighteen means I'm emancipated and free to make my own choices.

Today, with a clear mind and a clear path, I'm not concerned about what people think. Knowing Oliver loves me and the baby, I'm able to see our future. Companionship, love, working together as a family… like the Bravehearts… that's what I wanted all along.

With my life falling into place, I'm eager to see what the future holds.

Chapter Fifteen – The Bony Moon

The night of my birthday surprises me in many ways. Secretly, Hannah and Oliver arrange a party and invite my closest friends: Laurie, her mom, Carly, Gary, Sammie, and Charlie. However, the biggest surprise isn't the lemon-frosted chocolate cake that Oliver whipped up but the presence of my mom, dad, and little brother.

"Mom, why didn't you say something yesterday?" I tease her.

"It was a surprise!" She smiles and gestures toward my father like much has been accomplished with him being here.

Dad stands by the hors d'oeuvres, studying the olives and celery. I approach him, and he extends his arms for a hug. "I'm happy about your plans to marry Oliver. You're making a wise decision," he whispers.

I bite my lip. "Dad, it has nothing to do with wisdom. I love Oliver, and he loves me and the baby, period."

"So, the wedding will take place before the baby comes?" He raises both of his graying eyebrows to accentuate the question.

"No. It's impractical because of his classes… we want a

big wedding." I feel a warm hand touch mine, and glancing up, I see that my husband-to-be has joined us.

"Mr. Loveleigh, it's an honor to meet you." Oliver grips dad's hand and shakes it vigorously. "I love your daughter, and I've waited anxiously to ask for your blessing."

"Well, I… of course… you have my blessing." Dad nods his head without saying more. Apparently, Oliver's forthrightness and manners have impressed him.

My father's mellow attitude leaves me at a loss for words, but relief from the awkward pause quickly follows.

Colorful Charlie Quinn tosses his orange hair from his brow and cranks up the sound system that he brought to the party.

"Excuse us, Mr. Loveleigh." Oliver takes my hand.

"Let's dance, Nikki." My future husband puts his arm around my waist and guides me to an empty corner in the room. Locked together as close as my abdomen will allow, we sway to "Hold On" by Alabama Shakes.

This would be a perfect night to last forever.

* * * *

The Bravehearts, Oliver and I celebrate Oliver's nineteenth birthday and Christmas Eve with a private dinner before attending midnight mass at St. Teresa of Avila Catholic Church. It's so great that Oliver and I share December birthdays.

On the 24th, nineteen years ago, Hannah and Joe found a basket at their front door with a tiny baby boy wrapped in blankets. It just made sense to pick that day as his official birth date.

"He was the best gift that year!" Hannah bubbles with joy.

Tonight, in church, it doesn't bother me when people glance at my bountiful belly. I've accepted that God chose me to have this baby, at this particular time, in this particular way. I have faith that He has His reasons. In order for Oliver and I to have met, everything had to happen exactly the way that it did.

We sit in the third-row pew, center aisle. Oliver squeezes my hand, and I look up. Subtly, he motions with his head to the right. Darting my eyes, I see Joey Paul sitting a few seats over, and he signals his approval with a thumbs-up. Probably, some of the guys have told him of my plans to marry Oliver.

Acknowledging my friend, I smile and nod.

Open house on Christmas day brings food, music, presents, and a constant flow of guests invited by the Bravehearts. With Joe being one of the chiefs, I think the whole population of Qualla Boundary received invitations. The people laugh, tell stories, dance, eat, drink, and hug friends. It's a crazy joyful day.

Hannah prepares a delicious American Indian dish called poyha, which is ground venison baked in a cornmeal mixture with whole corn and grapes and served with fry bread. Another favorite is Hannah's yummy corn casserole. She sautés onions and celery, tears whole wheat bread for the bottom layer, adds cheese, the veggies, cream corn, and whole corn, then pours two eggs mixed with salt, tabasco and dry mustard on top.

Oliver and I take charge of baking Hannah's beloved cookie recipes: banana oatmeal, and feast day cookies with vanilla, pine nuts, and cinnamon. We laugh at our efforts and realize more dough clings to us than in the baking pans, but Hannah praises the tasty treats. "A cookie baked with love can never fail to taste good."

The guests parade in with gifts of puff-pastry apple pies, sour lemon cake, pumpkin muffins, and chocolate galore. We won't be lacking in desserts.

Joe's outside grill teases our appetites with the smoky aroma of wild rainbow trout, fresh flathead catfish, and venison steaks. There's no shortage of food, and people show their appreciation by asking for second and third helpings.

Earlier that morning, Oliver and I had exchanged small gifts. I tore into my neatly-wrapped box and was thrilled with a medallion of the Blessed Virgin Mary on a silver chain. Her arms were outstretched just like the first time I saw her at St. Teresa of Avila Church.

Oliver chuckled when he unwrapped his present, a silver medal of St. Christopher on a chain.

"St. Christopher will protect you while you're away at school," I said, and he responded by kissing me longer than he ever had before.

This evening, as the last group of guests say goodbye, large snowflakes fall from the sky and a chill fills the house. Joe and Oliver bring in dried oak logs and build a blazing fire in the stone fireplace. Sitting back in our chairs, close to the warm hearth, we reminisce about the day while digesting Christmas casseroles, grilled meats, cookies, pies, and cakes.

Why did I eat so much? And me, seven months pregnant.

* * * *

At my doctor's appointment, a few days after Christmas, Dr. Serrano cautions me for gaining a total of twenty pounds.

"You still have two months, Nikki. Better cut some calories so you won't have so much to lose after the baby's born."

Oliver glances at me and grins. "No more cookies."

Disgusted with myself, I frown and shake my head. "No more corn, cheese, or fry bread, either."

So, what does Hannah surprise us with at dinner? For dessert, she makes Oliver's favorite… Old Fashioned Indian Pudding… with cornmeal!

Oliver and I giggle, but I admit my tiny portion was heavenly.

The days fly by, and January 7th arrives way to soon. Oliver boards the shuttle to Asheville to catch his plane to New York.

My quiet tears whisper, *"I'll miss you. Come back soon."* Although, my heart thumps, *"Don't go. Stay with me and never leave."*

Oliver kisses my cheek and gently places his hand on my extended abdomen. "I plan to be with you in mid-February when Addie is born."

But Addie has different plans.

On January 31st, just before midnight, my water breaks and Hannah and Joe rush me to the hospital. After two hours of intense labor, a nurse holds the baby for me to see.

Squirming and screaming, the baby looks nothing like a spirit blossom. She's blood-red and has more black hair on her head than a bear cub. "5 lbs. 6 oz. and perfect," the doctor announces. "She's a little early, so as a precaution, we'll place her in the intensive care unit for a few hours."

Swooning from the ordeal, I just want to close my eyes.

* * * *

Awaking to beautiful cello music, my groggy eyes sweep to the left. Hannah sits next to the bed, with her belly still bulging. One of Oliver's recordings plays through her phone.

I appreciate her cheerful face, but her soft greeting sounds a little fuzzy. "Good morning, sweet one. You did it. You're the mother of a beautiful baby girl."

Sunlight streams through the hospital window, and I'm aware of yellow and red flowers on a credenza. Slowly, I continue studying the room and see my mother seated in an arm chair in the corner.

"Nikki, the baby is... lovely, dear, and already out of ICU." Mom approaches my bed. "How do you feel? Are you hungry? It's lunch time."

I attempt to sit up, but my woozy head forces me to lie back on my pillow. "I'm fine... I think. Maybe hungry."

Just then, a nurses' aid pops in with a food tray. "Let's raise you up a little." She presses a button, cranks my body to a sitting position, then slides the aromatic meal in front of me.

"It smells good. What is it?" I feel a little more like myself.

"Fried oysters." She smiles and leaves the room.

Staring at a seafood I've never eaten or cared to try, I get hungrier and hungrier. In spite of their known sliminess and the mysterious green stuff that fills their bellies, my mouth waters in anticipation of devouring the plump little mollusks.

"Oh dear, I can get you a sandwich from the snack bar. These small-town hospitals don't offer a choice of meals." Mom grabs her purse to go.

"No, mom. It's okay." I hoist the first oyster into my mouth and crunch while my mother gazes in disbelief. The second oyster follows and so on, until the plate is empty.

"I was starving." Picking up a napkin, I wipe crumbs from my mouth with satisfaction like fried oysters is my favorite meal.

Soon, Laura joins us. Between the three women, they wash my face, comb my hair, and trade my hospital garment for a pretty pink gown and robe to match.

"I spoke with Oliver. He's thrilled and wants you to call him when you're up to it." Hannah takes fuzzy slippers from my overnight bag and pushes them onto my feet.

"I want to see Addie." At this moment, I have only one thing on my mind.

"We can walk over to the nursery and peek in the window." Laura knows me well.

Throwing aside the bed covers, I attempt to stand, but a deep voice stops me.

"Hold on a minute. I knew you'd try to get up too soon. Here, try this." My dad and Bogey enter the room pushing a wheel chair.

With wobbly legs, I gladly accept his offer, and away we go.

My little baby girl steals our hearts, and we marvel at her rosebud mouth and petite nose. A nurse holds her to the window, and we count her tiny fingers and toes. Truly, a baby is a miracle, a gift from God.

Dad taps on the glass and makes kissy faces. A baby does that to people.

"Look at her teeny little fingernails!" My brother, who refers to himself as uncle Bogey, shakes a pink baby rattler from the hospital gift store.

Addie seems to respond by waving her arms and kicking her feet, and we all laugh.

In the early afternoon when things quiet down, the nurse

brings Addie to my room. Swaddling her in my arms, I notice her skin has toned to a smooth, light reddish-brown. With eyes as big as black olives, my baby girl grabs my index finger and coos. Instantly, I gain a mother's perspective.

Kachina Adsila… Spirit Blossom… the most beautiful baby in the world.

At that moment, I'm pulled to glance out the first-floor window. In a chestnut tree, about half way up, I spot a large, gray tabby cat that appears to be smiling. Kimi Wesa! Then… another figure materializes. It's Adawehi holding the secret feline.

My Cherokee angel beams with joy and his familiar melodies fill my head. After a minute of congratulatory nods, he and the cat fade away.

When the nurse comes to take Addie back to the nursery, I ask her the date of today.

"It's Tuesday, February 1st," she says.

Of course… February, the Bony Moon month.

After I nap and gain some of my strength, I call Oliver and share my experience of the past eighteen hours.

"I'm flying home tomorrow, and I can't wait to see my girls." Oliver's sweet words dance in my heart, and the enthusiasm in his voice ends another perfect day.

* * * *

After Oliver's visit, I settle into mothering my baby girl, and in a few days, Hannah's Tuwa arrives on schedule. We delight in sharing the experience of being moms together; nursing, diapering, exhaustion, and joyfulness make our days.

While the babies sleep, I study the Catechetics of the

Catholic Church. With Hannah's help, my instruction classes confirm my desire to become a member of St. Teresa of Avila Church.

During Oliver's Easter break, he travels home once more before our wedding and witnesses my confirmation ceremony.

At the Easter Vigil, I'm brought into the community of the Catholic Church. By the priest's words, I am reminded of my prior baptism, and my faith is renewed. My new life in Christ has begun, officially. The beautiful service ends with everyone making the sign of the cross, in the name of the Father, the Son, and the Holy Spirit.

Praise be to God!

Thank you, Mother Mary, for your intercessions.

Oliver, Hannah, and Joe embrace me; my catholic friends, Charlie and Joey Paul shake my hand. My parents grip my shoulders with an understanding hug and lightly kiss me on the cheek while Bogey eyeballs the proceedings with aloofness.

I catch his gaze and smile.

One of these days… little brother… one of these days…

Chapter Sixteen –
The Wedding

The next few weeks fly by, and my flawless wedding day finds me floating on air like a downy feather. The decorations, the clothes, the food, the bright blue sky, the subtle breeze, the mild temperature… everything is like a beautiful vision.

I'm marrying Oliver Rainchild. Good dreams really do come true!

Hannah and Joe have created a grand reception area on their landscaped yard. Containers of white roses, green plants, and blue/green hydrangeas accent the lush lawn. Turquoise streamers drape from trees to create an enchanted effect, and ivy trellises form imaginary walls.

My bridesmaids, Laura and Carly, pin the hair off my neck with borrowed pearl combs and slip a blue garter onto my thigh. They help me wriggle into my new off-shoulder, white satin wedding dress that is accented with lace and silk ribbons.

My loyal friends, dressed in frilly, turquoise chiffon, even mend a rip in my petticoat when I accidentally hang a heel.

"Wait. What do you have that's old?" Laura asks.

Giggling at her determination to follow tradition, I hold up my ring finger with the ancient turquoise stone. "This should do." I laugh, and my attendants laugh with me.

For the groom's assistants, Oliver selects two friends from the Qualla Boundary band. They clean up nicely in gray suits and Hannah's handmade ties, but no one outshines my handsome groom-to-be in his white tux and turquoise cummerbund.

The service takes place at St. Teresa of Avila Catholic Church. My mother and Mrs. Acres have decorated every inch of the sanctuary with large baskets of cut flowers from their gardens. Purple iris, pink camellias, yellow daffodils, and white baby's breath accent the church with brilliance. Red and white rose petals blanket the center aisle, and the mingled fragrances from all the flowers contribute to my dream state.

The guests have dressed in primary colors to witness the blessed marriage, and the colorful crowd overflows into the front vestibule. We have invited everyone we know in town and from the tribe, which is the Cherokee way.

My mom, tall in a navy and white stripe suit, holds Addie who behaves like a happy, four-month-old... no crying or fussing at her mom's wedding. Alert and wide-eyed, my baby girl pays attention to every aspect of the ceremony, especially when the flower girl tosses more rose petals.

With his head held high, my dad walks me down the aisle, arm in arm. My brother, the ringbearer, joins the procession with the curiosity of a young maternal uncle.

Bogey ponders the ornate church and pats the pocket that shields a silver wedding band inscribed with "I love you" and engraved with an eternity vine.

Joe stands faithfully by Oliver as his best man. Hannah, my matron of honor, clutches baby Tuwa in her arms. Although, Hannah's Qualla Boundary friends hover like a host of angels, ready to help in an instant.

After exchanging happy eyes and loving grins with my beloved Oliver, I glance down at my wedding bouquet. The cluster of red roses stand for love, and the cascading white roses suggest new beginnings. *How perfect for us!*

My promise to Oliver pledges my straight-forward, forever love, but Oliver's poetic vows dazzle me and our guests.

"She walks in beauty like the night..." He recites a poem by Keats, and then with a gleam in his eyes, he says a Cherokee Wedding Prayer:

"God in Heaven above, please protect the one I love.

We honor all You created as we pledge our hearts and lives together...

We honor Mother Earth... and ask for our marriage to be abundant...

We honor Fire... and ask for our union to be warm...

We honor Wind... and ask that we sail safely through life...

We honor Water... to clean and soothe our relationship...

With all the forces of the universe you created, we pray for harmony and true happiness, as we forever grow young together."

In a church filled with fresh flowers and stained-glass windows, the wall-mounted statues of Mary and Christ in His Passion, oversee our fairy-tale wedding, and the magnificence overwhelms me.

The magic continues through the "I do's," and when the priest says "Oliver, you may kiss your bride," I pray my shaky legs don't buckle.

Cameras flash and cell phones tap photo after photo, recording our bliss. Our official wedding photographer, Joey Paul, snaps and snaps until eventually everyone drifts to the Braveheart's house for the Cherokee part of the marriage, the reception, and more pictures.

At home, Oliver appears on the decked-our lawn, and a hush falls over the crowd. He's handsomely dressed in a traditional, suede wedding shirt accented with bright silk ribbons, turquoise beading, and tassels.

I hurry to my room, and with my bridesmaids' assistance, I prepare to astonish my new husband with *my* genuine Cherokee attire. Carly braids my hair into long plaits, and Laura secures a headband that Hannah created with turquoise, yellow and red beads.

Then, my two friends help me pull on my full-length "tear dress," so named from the Trail of Tears era when Cherokee women had no scissors to cut fabric.

The tribeswomen made their dresses from torn squares of cloth. This style of dress became synonymous with the Cherokee people, and they used it for all occasions, even weddings.

I am thankful that Hannah helped me sew my replica of a "tear dress." It features long bell sleeves, a wide-belted waist, and horizontal bands of bright ribbon on soft turquoise-colored fabric. Hannah's mother loans me the squash-blossom necklace made of silver and turquoise stones that completes my outfit.

I enter the garden amid whispers of admiration, and Oliver seems impressed by my authentic marriage apparel. Holding the Cherokee wedding bouquet of yellow roses mixed with white feathers, I feel surrounded by the joy and happiness that the two colors represent.

Our attendants take their places, and the ceremonial rites begin.

As presiding chief of the tribe, Joe Braveheart, lights the sacred fire pit. A Cherokee priest blesses us and chants a variation of the wedding prayer. The bride, me, faces the groom and offers bread, symbolizing my willingness to be a good homemaker. At the same time, Oliver presents a ham of venison to show he will provide for Addie and me.

Tribal dancers perform the circular stomp dance in a flurry of bouncing eagle feathers, swinging tassels, and tightly braided hair. Afterwards, some other Qualla Boundary guests sing Cherokee songs to welcome our family into the tribe.

At the end of the ceremony, a group of elders cover Oliver and me in a big white blanket to show our oneness. As a united couple, we drink herbal tea together from an antique wedding vase with double spouts. That's when good wishes, hugs, handshakes, and kisses begin. Congratulations overflow until the guests meander toward the buffet.

The caterer serves traditional Cherokee wedding food. Deer meat, turkey, and fish is prepared every way possible; baked, fried, kabobbed, and stewed. Bowls of succotash, bean dishes, corn on the cob, and fry bread tacos top the list. For dessert, American Indian sunflower cakes and Cherokee yam cakes win approval. Everything is eaten; nothing is wasted. *It's like Christmas over again.*

My mother receives compliments for creating the delicious, artistic multi-tiered wedding cake. On each layer, she depicts the flora and fauna that have special meaning to the Cherokee people. She uses frosting to fashion small native plants like white Rue Anemone for its medicinal purposes and yellow Trout Lily for its edible leaves. To represent the

Cherokee Nation's respect for the animal kingdom, mom has shaped tiny deer, eagles, and bears from earth-colored icing.

For music at the reception, dad has hired a local Cherokee band. They feature a musician who plays an American Indian love flute crafted from sacred, indigenous cedar wood.

Dancing the first dance, Oliver and I wrap around each other and sway to our favorite spiritual song, "Oceans," by Hillsong.

My husband gazes into my eyes. "I love you... more today than yesterday... if that's possible," he whispers.

I melt into buttery pancake syrup but quickly profess my love for him, too.

Dad and I two-step to the second song, and he apologizes for being uptight and prejudiced in the past.

He wanted me to always be his "little girl" just like I wanted him to always be "my daddy."

"You're forgiven, dad. I realize the circumstances caused your reaction. Let's set it all aside now and live for the future."

Oliver approaches with Addie in his arms and reclaims me. The three of us glide across the wooden dance platform constructed by Joe, and our baby girl coos with delight.

Sneaking away from the merrymakers, we put Addie to bed, but the celebration continues through the night, Cherokee style.

Sweet dreams, precious baby... my spirit blossom.

Nobody's Baby

Epilogue

In the fall, Oliver and I move to New York, into a student apartment, and meet other married couples, some with children. Our neighbor's mother keeps their baby and offers to watch Addie for a small fee. I pass my GED with flying colors, thanks to Hannah's home-school program, and start college classes right away in Columbia's off-campus program.

Hannah's vision of our girls aiding American Indian tribes stays on my mind. In fact, I have dreamed that Addie and Tuwa promote the reform of Indian treaties and protest the exploitation of resources on reservations.

In my wakeful state, I wonder if my dreams are influenced by Hannah's, or if they're prophesies?

* * * *

As the years roll by, Oliver works his way up to conductor of the New York Symphony Orchestra. I earn a PhD in Native American/Indian Studies and land a teaching position at Columbia University. My young hopes of a meaningful career have materialized but with one difference. My name is Dr. Nicole Rainchild.

Who knew I could have a family and a profession?

Oliver and I visit our families in North Carolina as often as possible, and Addie and Tuwa have become great friends. Addie loves spending summers and holidays on Cherokee land at Qualla Boundary with Hannah, Joe, and Tuwa. Of course, my parents absolutely adore their granddaughter and delight in spoiling her.

With Oliver adopting Addie legally and emotionally, he has raised her as his own child, the same as our twin boys, Christian and Joseph.

Some days, I think of the past and Adsila's biological father. However, I don't dwell on the thought that he was most likely Cherokee.

Addie and Tuwa have grown up to look alike with piercing dark eyes and thick black hair. They think alike, too. Both young women are passionate about majoring in Indian Studies at college. They have joined activists' groups and plan on attending law school with a focus on American Indian rights.

Maybe Hannah's dream and my dream will come true. Maybe our babies will shape a better future for all American Indian tribes. Perhaps, through their efforts, reservations will gain sovereignty. Better jobs will be created and lives will be saved from the cycle of poverty and everything that comes with it.

My desire to empower American Indian children with a better life will be fulfilled through my daughter and Hannah's daughter.

Thank you, Holy Spirit, for choosing me to raise Your spirit blossom, my Addie. Amen

Not the end... but the beginning of a humane future... for all people.

Glossary of Cherokee and American Indian Words

alone	u-wa-sa
ancient	ka-i-e-le
angel	a-da-we-hi
animal	ga-na-tla-i
baby	u-s-di
blossom	ad-si-la
butterfly	a-po-ni
cat	we-sa
come	e-he-na
cry	a-tlo-ya-s-di
December (Snowy Moon)	Qua-v-s-gi-ga
do	nah-dv-ga
earth	tu-wa
February (Bony Moon)	Ka-ga-li
fertile	u-dv-hi-s-di
ghost	a-s-gi-na
girl	a-ge-yu-tsa
go	a-ne-ga
healthy	do-hi

hello	a-si-yu
horse	so-qui-li
keep	hi-ne-yu
lost	u-le-nah-i-da
love	a-da-ga-u-e
married person	u-da-tli
May (planting moon)	A-na-a-gv-ti
newborn baby	u-s-di-u-da-ge-i
Nikki	Ni-ki
no	tla-no
no good	u-yo-i
not	na-s-gi
owl	u-gu-gu
pretty	u-wa-du-hi
secret	ki-mi
seeker of truth	du-yu-go-dv-a-yo-s-di
spirit	a-do-nv-do
spirit	ka-chi-na
who	ga-go
why	ga-do-no
wolf	wa-ya

Cherokee and American Indian words are shown phonetically.

Facts:

The eastern band of the Cherokee Nation owns an area called the Qualla Boundary in the foothills of the Great Smoky Mountains at Cherokee, North Carolina. The land was purchased in the 1800's and the federal government of the United States holds it in trust.

The Oconaluftee River runs through Qualla Boundary and is held sacred by the Cherokee people.

The Cherokee Lights and Legends event is a Christmas festival held every year at the Cherokee Indian Fair Grounds in Cherokee, N.C. For more info contact the Cherokee Welcome Center at 800-438-1601.

The U.S. government's passage of the Indian Removal Act in 1830 resulted in thousands of Cherokee, Muscogee, Seminole, Chickasaw, and Choctaw Indians dying in the relocation process forced upon them. The "Trail of Tears" phrase originated from the last removal of 16,000 Cherokee people from the southeastern United States in 1838. Approximately, 6,000 died of starvation, disease, and exposure while walking to their forced destination west of the Mississippi River.

The style of the "tear dress," so popular with Cherokee women even today, came from the "Trail of Tears" period. At that time, no scissors were available to make clothes because the people had their possessions taken away. They tore fabric instead of cutting it. The word *tear* can be pronounced as in "Trail of Tears" or as in torn material.

About the Author

Teresa J. Carson is a member of the Society of Children's Book Writers and Illustrators and a professional member of the Cat Writers Association. She has written two pre-teen books about a cat that has adventures in Italy, *Sofia's Angel* and *Sofia's Secret*.

Ms. Carson worked as a copywriter for radio and TV in Virginia and designed ads for a California newspaper. She studied art history at the University of Virginia, English composition at Piedmont Va. Community College, and travel writing and writing for children at Daytona State College.

Nobody's Baby, a coming-of-age, fictional tale for young adults, is laced with emotion, history, and hope for a better future for all American Indians.

Teresa and her husband, Walt, live in South Daytona, Florida with their two white cats.

Acknowledgements

A thousand thanks, *sowoiyagayvli wado*, to:

My editor and daughter, Stephanie Songchild, proprietor of Songbird Farm in Oregon, for her excellent editing. Her talent and ability is unending!

My husband, Walter Lee Andrews, guitarist, singer, and songwriter, for his support and suggestions. His gifts are amazing!

My granddaughter, Haley Songchild, author of *Fairy Dust, The Milowa Plains,* and *Orcali Child.* Her creativity inspires me!

My devoted fans, for encouraging me to keep writing. Inspiration for *Nobody's Baby* came from my constant guide and teacher, the Holy Spirit, whom I met in the Adoration Chapel of Epiphany Church.

TJC
South Daytona, Florida
June 15, 2019

www.ingramcontent.com/pod-product-compliance
Lightning Source LLC
Chambersburg PA
CBHW031318040426

42443CB00005B/125